Interviewer's Manual

revised edition

Survey Research Center

Institute for Social Research

The University of Michigan
Ann Arbor

ISR Code No. 3794

Library of Congress Catalog Card No. 76-630039
ISBN 0-87944-194-1 paperbound
ISBN 0-87944-195-X clothbound

Published by the Institute for Social Research
The University of Michigan, Ann Arbor, Michigan 48106

First Published 1969, Revised Edition 1976
Second Printing 1978
© 1976 The University of Michigan, All Rights Reserved
Printed in the United States of America

Cover Design by Wallaby Inc., Ann Arbor, Michigan

STATEMENT OF PROFESSIONAL ETHICS

All interviewers for the Survey Research Center are expected to understand that their professional activities are directed and regulated by the following statements of policy:

The Center undertakes a study only after it has been evaluated in terms of its importance to society and its contribution to scholarly knowledge. It does not conduct studies which are, in its opinion, trivial, of limited importance, or which would involve collecting information that could be obtained more easily by other means, and it does not undertake secret research or conduct studies for the sole benefit of one individual, company, or organization. The Center is a community of scholars whose findings are available to everyone. Every effort is made to disseminate research results as widely as possible; this is done through books, journal and magazine articles, news releases, papers presented at professional meetings, and in the classroom.

The rights of human subjects are a matter of primary concern to the Center and all study procedures are reviewed to ensure that individual respondents are protected at each stage of research. While it is the Center's policy to make study findings public, the utmost care is taken to ensure that no data are released that would permit any respondent to be identified. All information that links a particular interview to a specific respondent is removed as soon as the interview is received at the Center; this information is maintained in special confidential files while the study is in progress, and is destroyed after the study closes. Interviews themselves are identified only by numbers.

The Center's strict precautions to protect the anonymity of respondents will be undermined if the interviewer does not treat information concerning respondents with equal regard. Interviewers perform a professional function when they obtain information from individuals in personal interviews, and they are expected to maintain professional ethical standards of confidentiality regarding what they hear and observe in the respondent's home. All information about respondents obtained during the course of the research is privileged information, whether it relates to the interview itself or includes extraneous observations concerning the respondent's home, family, and activities.

TABLE OF CONTENTS

CHAPTER 1 — THE SAMPLE SURVEY   1

  What Kinds of Questions Are Asked?   1
  When Is a Survey Made?   1
  How Is Survey Information Used?   1
  Types of Surveys   2
  Conducting a Survey   2
  Careful Study Procedures   5

CHAPTER 2 — INTRODUCTION TO THE INTERVIEW   7

  Initial Contact   7
  Securing the Interview   7

CHAPTER 3 — USING THE QUESTIONNAIRE   11

  Center Questionnaires   11
  Asking the Questions   11
  Clarifying the Respondent's Role by Using Positive Feedback   13

CHAPTER 4 — PROBING AND OTHER INTERVIEWING TECHNIQUES   15

  Kinds of Probes   15
  Nondirective Probing   16
  Examples of Probes   17

CHAPTER 5 — RECORDING AND EDITING THE INTERVIEW   19

  Questionnaire Format and Conventions   19
  Rules for Recording Responses   20
  Tips on Note Taking   21
  Mechanics of Recording and Editing Interviews   22
  The Thumbnail Sketch   23
  Summary Tips on Editing   25
  Examples of Recorded Responses   25
  Tape Recording Interviews   25

Illustrations

  5-1 Example of Completed Questionnaire Page   24
  5-2 Example of Completed Questionnaire Page   26
  5-3 Example of Completed Questionnaire Page   27

CHAPTER 6 — CALL AND CALL-BACK STRATEGY   29

  Suggested Procedures   29
  Reluctant Respondents   30

CHAPTER 7 — TELEPHONE INTERVIEWING (REINTERVIEWING) — 33

Telephone Interviewing Techniques — 33

CHAPTER 8 — SAMPLING PRINCIPLES AND PROCEDURES — 35

Sampling — A Definition — 35
Survey Research Center Sampling — 35
The Interviewer and the Sample — 37
Summary — 37

Illustrations

8-1 SRC Sampling Method — 36

CHAPTER 9 — TYPES OF LIVING QUARTERS DEFINED — 39

Housing Units — 39
Excluded Quarters — 40
Unclassified Quarters — 40

CHAPTER 10 — SCOUTING THE CHUNK — 41

Segment Identification — 41
Become Familiar with the Map — 41
Know the Housing Unit Definition — 42
Check the Boundaries — 42
Indicate Internal Features — 44
Choose the Listing Procedure to Use — 44
Special Cases — Apartment Buildings — 45
Special Cases — Excluded Quarters — 46
Area Procedure — 47
Building Listing Procedure — 59

Illustrations

10-1   Chunk Sketch Showing Man-Made Features as Boundaries — 42
10-2a   Chunk Sketch as It Appears When Sent for Scouting — 43
10-2b   Chunk Sketch after Interviewer Has Made Inquiries — 44
10-3a   Building Listing Showing Floors of Apartment Building — 45
10-3b   Interviewer's Sketch of Apartment Floor Arrangement — 46
10-4   Chunk Sketch Showing Use of Imaginary Boundaries — 48
10-5   Chunk Sketch Showing Use of Odometer Readings to Pinpoint Boundaries — 49
10-6   Transmittal Form — 51
10-7   Portion of Field Map Locating Chunk 8005 — 52
10-8   Front Side of Information Sheet as Received — 53
10-9   Chunk Sketch as Received — 54
10-10   Information Sheet Completed (Front) — 55
10-10b Information Sheet Completed (Back) — 56
10-11   Chunk Sketch Completed — 57
10-12   Interviewer's Sketch of Trailer Park — 58
10-13   Chunk Sketch for Building Listing — 60

10-14a Completed Building Listing	61
10-14b Completed Building Listing	62
10-14c Completed Building Listing	63

CHAPTER 11 — LISTING AND UPDATING DURING THE INTERVIEWING PERIOD — **65**

Materials	65
Procedures for Listing in Sample Segments	77
Types of Living Quarters	80
Guidelines for Listing	83
Completing Sampling Forms	83
Perfecting the Sample Listing	86

Illustrations

11-1 Blue Folder Cover — Area Segment	67
11-2 Chunk Sketch — Area Segment	68
11-3 Segment Listing 6003B — Take-All Segment	69
11-4 Segment Listing 6003A — Take-Part Segment	70-71
11-5 Inside Spine and Back Cover of Blue Folder	72
11-6 Back of Blue Folder	73
11-7 Blue Folder Cover — Building Segment	74
11-8 Building Listing Sheet	75
11-9 Segment Listing 6003E — Take-Part Segment	76
11-10 Several HU's in a Building	80
11-11 Sample Address Summary Form	85
11-12 Situations Requiring Adding HU's to Segment Listing Sheet	88
11-13 Listing Problems You May Encounter During Interviewing	89

CHAPTER 12 — CHOOSING RESPONDENTS — **91**

Identifying Occupied Housing Units	91
Selecting the Respondent	92
Nonresponse Classification	97

Illustrations

12-1 Determining Members of the Household	93
12-2 Respondent Selection by Family Relationship	96
12-3 Respondent Selection Using Selection Table	98

CHAPTER 13 — OFFICE FORMS AND RECORDS — **101**

Time Sheet	101
Mileage Statement	102
Travel Expense Report (TER)	102
Payroll Practices	111

Illustrations

13-1 Time Sheet	103-104
13-2 Mileage Statement	105-106
13-3 Travel Expense Report	107-108

CHAPTER 14 — ADMINISTRATIVE PROCEDURES — 113

    Communication — 113
    Supervisors and Field Coordinators — 114
    Study Procedures — 115
    Study Materials — 118
    Evaluation of Interviewers — 120

Illustrations

    14-1 Progress Report — 119
    14-2 Project Completion Form — 121
    14-3 Coder's Report — 122
    14-4 Respondent Evaluation Letter — 123-124
    14-5 Evaluation Sheet for Pay Rate Change — 127-128
    14-6 Observation Interview Report — 129-130

APPENDIX A — TABLE FOR COMPUTING PERCENTAGES — 131-132

APPENDIX B — PRETESTING — 133

    Pretesting in the Field — 133
    The Debriefing — 134
    Pretesting Elites — 135

APPENDIX C — LETTER TO AUTHORITIES — 137

APPENDIX D — TAPE-RECORDED INTERVIEW EVALUATION CODE — 139

INDEX — 141

1 THE SAMPLE SURVEY

A survey usually involves collecting data by interviewing a sample of people selected to represent accurately the population under study. Each person in the sample is asked the same series of questions, and responses are then organized so that conclusions can be drawn from them. This information is used either to solve a particular problem or to add needed information about the problem.

Precise interviewing procedures are used to ensure full and accurate data collection. If careful methods are used, then the data gathered from a sample of respondents can be used confidently to represent the total population. Using an accurate "sample," it is possible to avoid the very expensive and time-consuming procedure of taking a census, which involves a complete accounting of every person in the population being studied.

WHAT KINDS OF QUESTIONS ARE ASKED?

Survey questions concern people's behavior, their attitudes, how and where they live, and information about their backgrounds (demographic data), as indicated below.

- **Behavior.** Many survey questions relate to the actions or behavior of people in various areas of human activity. In the economic area, for example, patterns of spending and saving have been studied intensively in surveys. In other areas, such behaviors as voting, reading, visits to the doctor, geographical movements, and recreational habits are subjects of inquiry.

- **Attitudes.** Some survey questions concern people's opinions, attitudes, and expectations. These are areas in which it is unlikely that data would be available from nonsurvey sources.

- **Environment.** In many surveys it is important to have data about the circumstances in which respondents live in order to interpret their responses more accurately. This includes information about the neighborhood, the adequacy of living quarters, membership in groups and organizations, and so on.

- **Personal descriptive (demographic) data.** Surveys always include questions regarding the sex, age, occupation, income, education, and other personal-social characteristics of respondents. By gathering this kind of information we are able to make statements about the similarities or differences among people in different age groups, occupational groups, educational groupings, etc. For instance, we can find out how many people aged 20-29 own cars, and how car owners in this age group compare with those in other age groups. Certain kinds of demographic data are more significant in one area of research than in others. For example, it is more important to know about a respondent's nationality and where he grew up in an election study than it is in an economic study.

Several questions in each of these categories usually appear in every SRC questionnaire.

WHEN IS A SURVEY MADE?

Surveys are taken when the desired information cannot be obtained more accurately and less expensively in other ways. For example, it would be inefficient to conduct a sample survey to determine the number of automobiles in use in the United States. This information may be obtained more quickly and reliably by studying the files of state licensing bureaus. But a survey would be required to obtain certain information about autos. For instance, no recorded information is available on the occupations, buying intentions, driving habits, or other characteristics of automobile owners. The automobile plays a large part in the economy of the nation and such information is of value not only to car manufacturers, but also to agencies responsible for city planning, highway departments, and travel and recreation agencies. To talk to every car owner in the United States would be prohibitively expensive and time consuming, but it would be feasible to talk to a sample of car owners.

HOW IS SURVEY INFORMATION USED?

After gathering various kinds of information, the study director is then in a position to analyze the data and investigate the problem. He or she will be concerned with such matters as how many, who, how, and why. A survey on the use of public libraries, for instance, might be designed to answer questions like these:

How many people use a public library more than five times a year?

Who are the people who tend to use public libraries (by age, occupation, etc.)?

How do people make use of a public library (for pleasure, reference, etc.)?

Why do some people use public libraries while others do not?

The answers to such questions are of interest to many people. For example, librarians, educators, and publishers would find them useful when they consider the practical problems of improving facilities. They might also be useful to theoretical researchers interested in studying the manner in which the public is reached and influenced by information from various sources.

After the survey data have been analyzed, a report is prepared which is generally published and made available to the public. The survey results can then be used as a basis for changing, improving, or even discarding existing procedures. Survey data are also used by other researchers to increase their knowledge of a field or to define new areas for investigation.

TYPES OF SURVEYS

Library use is only one example of the many topics which can be studied through the survey method. Today, the survey is being used to advantage in opinion polling, market research, census taking, and social research. These types of surveys and the various ways in which they are used are described briefly below:

• **The public opinion poll.** Opinion polls are perhaps the most well-known among the various types of surveys. The polls are an outgrowth of the "straw" or informal surveys conducted by newspapers as early as 1824 for the purpose of forecasting elections. During the 1930's, a number of independent polling agencies were organized; among them were Roper and Gallup. Since then, these organizations have polled public opinion on elections, public affairs, and other specific topics of interest. These "straw vote" polls have aroused much popular interest in survey work.

• **The market research survey.** Another type of survey activity is carried on by businesses in consumer market research. Each year, a great many surveys are conducted by market research groups to determine consumer needs and the effectiveness of marketing programs. Market surveys focus on consumers' attitudes toward current products as well as on possible demand for new products.

• **The descriptive statistical survey.** This kind of survey is conducted largely by the government to obtain major descriptive information about the population, its density, the composition of the labor force, national health statistics, and so forth. From earliest times, governments have taken inventories of their human resources for taxation, military, and legislative purposes. In addition, democratic procedures in government brought forth a need for better communication between people and their officials. Government agencies such as the Census Bureau conduct or sponsor a wide variety of surveys designed to measure public opinion and gather statistics.

• **The survey for social research.** The social survey is a major research method used by social scientists to gather and analyze information about the social and economic conditions of the population or segments of the population. This information leads to a better understanding of human beings in their social setting.

Social surveys are an outgrowth of the European social reform movements of the 19th century. In France, England, and other countries, philanthropists and others interested in social welfare began to study prison conditions, the treatment of mental patients, poverty, and other social problems. These early studies were based on the idea that until the extent and nature of these problems could be measured, very little effective action could be taken to improve conditions.

The European survey movement spread rapidly to the United States after 1900. The problems of the many ethnic groups in this country and the special social problems of large cities were obvious fields for investigation. The number of social surveys has increased steadily since 1915; they deal with such things as education, care of mental patients, housing, public health, and crime. The Depression and two World Wars, which brought nationwide social and economic problems, were also factors in the development of the social survey movement.

Clearly, the only way to find out how people feel and what their opinions are is to ask them directly, and the best way to do this is through a survey. Survey procedures in earlier days tended to be haphazard and impractical. Over the years, through experimentation and experience, researchers have developed more scientific and systematic methods. Developments in social science and statistics were instrumental in speeding their progress. Researchers realized that they could reliably estimate conditions in large populations by carefully observing relatively small numbers of people.

CONDUCTING A SURVEY

To the casual observer, conducting a survey may appear to be a simple procedure. The questions seem obvious enough and the tabulated percentage of responses adds up to one hundred. The casual observer seldom suspects the detailed labors which lie behind the neat columns of figures in the final report. The fact is that a survey must be carried out, step by step, with the utmost care.

Just as a chemist must follow a chemical formula precisely in order to make the desired product, so the researcher must follow the survey formula precisely in order to produce accurate information. Each person involved in the survey process must carry out his own work accurately and must work with others as a member of a team if the survey is to be successful.

Information about the steps involved in conducting a survey should help interviewers understand the importance of their role in the entire process. Here are eight steps the Survey Research Center follows for most surveys:

1. Defining the study objectives;
2. Choosing the study design;
3. Selecting the sample;
4. Constructing and pretesting the questionnaire;
5. Interviewing the respondents;
6. Coding the interviews;
7. Tabulating and analyzing the results;
8. Writing the study report.

Let us examine each of these steps separately.

Defining the study objectives. A first step in any survey is to define and outline the area under investigation. In doing this, the study planners work out a statement of the problem and the general objectives of the survey. These general objectives are then broken down into specific objectives, and a list of "specifications of data" is made. This list states the specific items of information which will be needed in order to solve the problem, and forms the basis for the questionnaire.

Determining the specific objectives of the survey involves considerable planning. The researchers must analyze their problem carefully to see what part of it can best be explored by taking a survey and what parts are more suitable for other methods of research. In some cases, the study planners need to go into the field for group or informal exploratory interviews to help determine some of the important factors in the investigation.

Suppose we consider the problem of conducting a survey on public attitudes toward taxes. It is necessary to define the problem by specifying what types of taxes the survey will cover. Federal tax? State and local tax? Income tax? Sales tax? The survey may deal with all or only some of these. The researchers must first acquaint themselves thoroughly with the tax structure, laws and forms, as well as with any previous research done on the subject, and perhaps study public reactions to the tax forms or dates and methods of payment.

Also, it might be necessary to know how much the public knows about taxes. Do they know what the tax rates are? Do they know what the money is used for? Would they be willing to see public services curtailed for the sake of reducing taxes? If so, would they want all public services curtailed, or just some? Which ones?

The planners of the survey must consider all aspects of the problem. Perhaps they will not be able to deal with all of them because of limited time or money, so that the scope of the survey will have to be limited. In any case, the goal is to specify what aspects of the subject will be covered, and to anticipate exactly the type of findings that will be included in the final study report.

Choosing the study design. Most studies require a single survey of one particular group of people. But surveys may be designed in a variety of other ways, depending upon the objectives of the study. It may be desirable, for some purposes, to survey contrasting groups (parents, students, and teachers for example) or similar groups (a dozen residential areas or six automotive plants), and to compare the sets of findings. In studies in which it is important to measure changes or trends in opinion or behavior, a group of people may be selected as respondents, and this group may be interviewed several times at specific intervals. Groups of respondents like these are called "panels."

Selecting the sample. Another basic step in planning a survey is to determine the sample to be used in the study, or exactly what group of people should be investigated. A sample is a small part of the total population carefully selected to represent that population. The people selected as the sample (to be interviewed as our respondents) are chosen by precise mathematical procedures so that the information obtained from them can be generalized to the total population.

The population to be sampled is called the "universe." If the survey objectives involve studying the opinions of the American people, the total group to be studied may be defined as the entire adult population of the country living in housing units. The study must define what it means by "adults"; this is usually all persons age 18 and over. The sample selection process must give each member of the population a known chance to be selected for the sample. In some cases, the survey objectives may be concerned only with a particular company or plant, so that the universe consists only of the employees within the organization. In these cases, a sample could be selected to represent each level within the company, from unskilled workers to executive staff.

Many of SRC's surveys involve a study of the entire American adult population. For this reason, the Center maintains a national sample of primary areas which have been carefully chosen to represent the total national population.

Once the basic choices of the population and sample size have been made, the next step is to select the actual housing units to be contacted. Using a method which will be covered in the chapters on sampling, the Center's Sampling Section draws a sample of housing units within each primary area in the survey. Particular individuals at the selected addresses then comprise the sample of respondents for the study.

Constructing and pretesting the questionnaire. When the study planners have listed the information they need from respondents, they are ready to start building the questionnaire.

This involves many considerations. The researchers must word the questions so that they will be understood clearly. They must arrange them in the best possible order so that the questions follow each other naturally. The questions should be capable of eliciting objective answers, and should not be biased in any direction. The questionnaire must also be of a reasonable length.

Before a questionnaire is used in the field, it undergoes extensive pretesting to determine whether:

- All important phases of the survey have been adequately covered.
- The questionnaire stimulates respondent cooperation.
- The questions flow smoothly.
- The questions are completely understood by the respondents.
- The questions elicit responses that are in line with the objectives of the survey.

The study director's staff, members of the Field Office staff, and several experienced interviewers serve as pretesters. These people conduct interviews with an appropriate group of people, then gather to discuss their experiences. On the basis of their observations, the questionnaire may be revised, some questions may be dropped and others substituted, new questions may be added, and others may be reworded or rephrased.

The revised version of the questionnaire is then tested again, and any other necessary revisions are made. Some questions which have been used for many years to measure changes in attitude from one survey to the next are not revised so that the measure will be consistent, but they are included in the pretest to check flow and timing.

The Field Office has one final step to identify problem areas in a questionnaire. Interviewers who work on a study are asked to take a "practice interview" with a respondent whom they do not know, prior to a study's starting date. This interview is a training session for the interviewer; it ensures that the interviewer understands the objectives of the questions, and it enables the study director and staff to clear up any misunderstandings or problems which were missed in pretesting.

Interviewing. The precise methods to be followed in administering the questionnaire are outlined in a book of instructions to the interviewer. This instruction book, written especially for each study, tells the interviewer about:

- The background, sponsoring organization, and general aims of the survey.
- The sampling procedures and whom to interview.
- The objective of each question or set of questions.
- Miscellaneous instructions on the field process such as the time schedule for the study, call procedures, etc.

Other materials to be used for interviewing in the field are also provided at this stage of the operation. These usually include field sampling materials, letters for respondents, and news releases for local newspapers.

At this point, the success of the survey rests in the hands of the interviewers. Throughout the interviewing period, the Field Office and the supervisors keep in close touch with the interviewers; the three-way communication among them must work at top efficiency during this stage.

When an interview has been completed and edited, the interviewer mails it to the Field Office. The Field Office has a master sample book for each study which contains a complete list of all housing units that have been selected for interviewing. As each interview arrives in the office, it is checked off in the master sample book so that at the end of the study there is a complete record of the entire sample. The study is not considered complete until every sample listing is accounted for by either an interview or a non-interview. Anything which reveals the address or identity of a housing unit, however, is removed or separated from the interview and kept inaccessible to unauthorized persons. Our guarantee of confidentiality to our respondents is upheld every step of the way.

Coding the interviews. A single study sometimes produces hundreds of thousands of words. In order to analyze this large body of material, the study director and his staff construct a "code."

The code can be used to transform this vast amount of information into a form that can be counted, measured, compared, and analyzed. One or more numeric codes are assigned to each of the respondent's answers and used to tabulate the survey results. Some codes are very simple; for example, "YES" is coded 1 and "NO" is coded 5. Other responses, particularly those for open-ended questions, may have many pages of possibilities which the coder must look through to find the closest fit. Codes for new questions are constructed from actual responses to the first production interviews, as well as from responses to pretest interviews.

It is very important to stick to a predetermined schedule of operations to ensure that the data flow is smooth for each procedure. During the first week of a study, while interviewing is getting started in the field, the analysis staff is building the code and training coders. Generally, production coding begins by the end of the second week of a study period; coders start work on interviews that have been sent in. With so many interviews which must be processed in the Field Office, it is necessary to maintain a steady flow of work to the coders, who are also working toward a deadline.

Tabulating and analyzing the results. When the respondents' answers have been coded into numbers, these are then transferred onto IBM punch cards. The information on these cards is then transferred to tapes and fed into computers which read the information on the tapes to compute statistics and print out data.

Writing the study report. Using elaborate statistical analyses, the analyst can construct tables of findings and arrive at conclusions, or at least draw implications, concerning the problem being studied. Reports written about the study contain these findings, a description of the methods used, a description of the survey sample, and statistical data.

CAREFUL STUDY PROCEDURES

Obviously the Survey Research Center must follow very careful procedures, and each member of the survey staff — sampler, interviewer, coder, and analyst — must carry out his or her own job thoroughly and accurately if any survey is to be a success.

The unhappy consequences of unsound sampling procedures are illustrated by the well-known prediction of the *Literary Digest* poll of the 1936 presidential election. The sample used by the *Digest,* which was supposed to represent all of the voters, was taken from such sources as lists of people who had telephones. People in the lower income levels who did not have phones and who tended to vote *against* Landon were not represented adequately, and the poll was self administered, so that many more Republicans than Democrats returned their questionnaires. Consequently, the *Digest* poll predicted that Landon would win by a landslide!

The interviewer must also be provided with well-designed field materials. The questionnaire, for example, needs to be worded carefully and tested out before it is used. One possible result of inadequate pretesting is humorously illustrated by a response to a question from a study of service veterans. The study was interested in veterans' experiences before they went into service as well as during the time they were in service. The question was, "What did you do right before you went into the service?" On the first pretest a respondent said, "Lady, you shouldn't ask me what I did *right* before I went into the service, you should ask me what I did *wrong!*" When the word "right" was changed to "just," the question still met the study objectives without the likelihood of being misinterpreted by an unknown number of respondents.

The Center survey also requires that the interviewer proceed with a scientific attitude; your likes and dislikes should never influence your performance. Researchers cannot rely on guesses; they must collect their information carefully, and measure, weigh, and test for accuracy.

We have described the steps in the survey process in a general way. The two steps in which you will be intimately involved — *sampling* and *interviewing* — are discussed in detail in the next chapters.

2 INTRODUCTION TO THE INTERVIEW

Before a study goes into the field, a form letter signed by the Director of the Survey Research Center is sometimes sent to each respondent address. The letter briefly states that the Survey Research Center is conducting a survey and that a trained, professional interviewer will call at that address.

You are the "trained, professional interviewer" mentioned in the respondent letter. You must explain the nature of the study, the purpose of survey research, and the reason why you are standing at the respondent's door. Your interest in people and thorough knowledge of the instructions which you receive in training will make the task an easy one in most cases, but an interviewer must bring all of her* intuition and intelligence into play when someone in the household opens the door.

INITIAL CONTACT

There are two stages in a typical introductory situation. The first one occurs at the door when you make contact with the people living in the household; the second stage occurs when you are inside the house and able to talk more easily. The reaction of the person who answers the door is likely to be a mixture of curiosity and formal courtesy.

This initial interest will give you time to establish your identity by showing your ID card, and to allay any fears that you are a salesperson, bill collector, or any other sort of stranger with whom the householder might not wish to speak. In addition to the ID card which shows that you are an employee of The University of Michigan's Survey Research Center, you will also carry a blue folder with the University seal embossed on the cover. You will find it useful to carry extra copies of the respondent letter, current newspaper clippings about the Center's work, copies of reports to respondents on earlier studies, and other materials that demonstrate how our findings are used, the importance of our work, and the integrity of the Center's surveys.

The doorway is not a very convenient place to carry on a conversation, and the doorstep introduction should be just long enough to get you inside the house. Once you are inside, you will be in a better position to convince the person of the value of his cooperation. It is easier for the respondent to say "No, thank you" at the door than it is in the living room.

At the doorstep, you should state the course of action which you desire rather than ask permission for the interview. For instance, instead of asking, "May I come in?" — to which a respondent could easily reply "No" — say, "I would like to come in and talk with you about this." Avoid questions such as, "Are you busy now?" or "Could I take this interview now?" or "Should I come back?" Questions which permit undesired responses can lead or even push a respondent into refusing to be interviewed.

You should assume the respondent is *not* busy and approach the meeting as though the interview were going to take place right then — at the time of contact. Of course, if the respondent really is unavailable for an interview, by all means make arrangements to return at a more convenient time.

The first few contacts with a respondent should be personal ones, and not made by telephone. It is much easier for a respondent to say "no" and hang up the phone than it is to say "no" when you are standing in front of him. (The exceptions to this are telephone surveys and panel studies for which you call to make an appointment for the reinterview.)

The person who answers the door may not be the person you must interview. You should establish a cooperative relationship with whomever answers the door so that you will be able to obtain the information you need to select the respondent.

SECURING THE INTERVIEW

The most successful interviewer is one who is able to size up the situation quickly on the basis of what little information is available and to act accordingly. Approach each person who answers the door as if he were friendly and interested. Vary your approach in accordance with your intuitive feelings about the person. Some respondents will be quite willing to be interviewed with only a brief explanation of your purpose; for others you will need to go into some detail.

Remember not to be too specific about the interview in introducing yourself and the survey to the respondent. It is important that you avoid introducing a bias into the interview which might predispose the respondent to answer in a particular way. Very general statements such as: "We are interested in how people are getting along these days" or "We're talking to people all over

---

*Throughout this manual, the interviewer is always referred to as "she" and the respondent is referred to as "he." This does not mean that all of our interviewers are women or that all of our respondents are men. Actually, more than 50 percent of our respondents on national cross-section studies are women, as are the majority of our interviewers.

the country to see how they feel things are going in the world today" are usually quite successful. There is often a brief introductory statement printed on the front of the questionnaire which you can use.

Respondents have various kinds of concerns and questions, and you must be prepared to give correct and courteous answers, phrased so that they seem to be a natural part of your introductory conversation.

Here are some questions respondents are likely to ask, along with some suggested answers:

Q: *How did you happen to pick me? Who gave you our name?*

A: You see, in trying to find out what people in this country think, we cannot talk with everyone, but we try to talk to men and women of different ages in all walks of life. This is what we mean when we say 'cross-section.' We start by selecting certain counties and cities from all over the country (you can show the respondent the map on the back of a thank you card). In each of the areas the Center selects smaller areas such as blocks and then within each such area, specific addresses. Then, when the interviews from all these addresses are combined, we have opinions from a cross-section of people. (To emphasize our policy of confidentiality, it is important to tell the respondent that we have not chosen him by name; his address was chosen because it happened to be within preselected geographic boundaries. It might be appropriate to remind him that the respondent letter was sent to "Residents of the Household" and not to a name at that address.)

Q: *I really don't know anything about this.*

A: We are interested in your *opinions*, not in what information you may or may not have about the topics in the survey. I really think you will find the interview interesting and enjoyable. In a study such as this there are no right and wrong answers; we are simply interested in learning about your experiences and how you feel about things.

Q: *Why don't you go next door?*
Why don't you talk to my wife; she knows more about this than I do.

A: It would be nice if we could just interview the people we catch at home when we call, but that wouldn't give us a cross-section — we'd probably have too many housewives and older married people and not enough single people and working men. (It is quite natural for the respondent to feel unsure; he may be uncertain about the interviewing process or lack knowledge about the topic. These are two quite different concerns and you will learn to recognize them and deal with them accordingly. In both cases, however, you must reassure the respondent in order to allay his fears. Since you are talking to the selected respondent, it is his opinions which are important, and the sampling procedure does not permit you to "go next door" unless, of course, that address has also been selected. By the same token, it does not permit you to talk to his wife.)

Q: *What's this all about, anyway?*

A: We'll be talking about several things of current interest, such as the recreational facilities in this area, women's roles in society, and how you feel about the government. (An expansion of the introductory remarks should be adequate if you think that this question means just what it says. If, however, the respondent is voicing suspicion about the legitimacy of your visit, you might suggest that he call the Better Business Bureau or another local official with whom you are registered who can vouch for the fact that you are from a recognized organization known to be working on a survey in the area.)

Q: *What good will this do?*

A: (This is perhaps one of the most difficult questions to answer. While a survey which adds to our knowledge about problems and concerns in society is valuable, a particular study will probably have little or no direct effect on individual respondents.

This is a good time to bring out clippings from past studies, taken from both newspapers and periodicals such as *Time, Newsweek, The Wall Street Journal*, etc., and show the respondent how the information is used.

It may help if you explain that informed decisions are better than good guesses, and that government leaders and other decision-makers need the kind of information which can be obtained only by talking to people and finding out how they feel in order to formulate intelligent policies.)

Introduction to the Interview

Q: *What's The University of Michigan doing way out here in _____?*

A: The University has interviewers in 74 sample locations scattered throughout the country. I'm a local resident employed by The University of Michigan to do interviewing in this area. (Respondents often think you have come straight from Ann Arbor and, while this may be flattering, they will probably be reassured to know that you are a local resident. Our studies are often reported with an Ann Arbor dateline in national and local newspapers. This is another opportunity to show the respondent some of the current clippings or news releases which describe the way in which information is used — these will also show him that individual respondents are not mentioned or identified in any way.)

Your own state of mind is often reflected in the respondent's reaction to the request for an interview. If your approach is uncertain or uneasy, if you cannot answer the questions the respondent asks and seem vague about the work and its purposes, this feeling will be communicated to the respondent and he will react accordingly. If you have a pleasant, positive, and well-informed approach, this again will be reflected in the respondent's attitude. Both your effectiveness and your own satisfaction with your work will be increased by the knowledge that the job you are doing is legitimate and important, and by knowing what you are doing and how it should be done.

Remember that you have a right to ask a person for information, just as the respondent has a right to refuse to answer. In many homes you will be welcome because you represent a change in the day's routine. Most people enjoy being interviewed and many develop interest and insight into matters which they have not thought about before or thought about in the same way.

3 USING THE QUESTIONNAIRE

Your goal is to collect accurate information by using the survey questionnaire in accordance with sound interviewing practices. In order to fulfill this goal, you must know some basic facts about the Center's questionnaires and how they are used.

CENTER QUESTIONNAIRES

These questionnaires are designed to obtain accurate and complete information. They do this by meeting two criteria:

- **The research objectives of the study.** The study staff decides what pieces of information they need in order to fulfill the purposes of the study. They then design questions which they believe will be effective in obtaining the needed information.

- **Providing a uniform stimulus.** The researcher needs to combine and to analyze statistically the data collected in all of the interviews. This means that the data must be collected in a uniform manner from all respondents, and all of the people in a sample must be asked the same questions in the same way.

Responses are strongly influenced by the way in which a question is worded. Obviously, if a question is worded differently for different respondents, it will not produce comparable results among interviews. Question order must also be the same from interview to interview because changes in sequence affect respondents' answers. Finally, each SRC interviewer is part of a large group of interviewers all across the country. It is only when each interviewer uses the questionnaire in the same fashion as all other interviewers that we can hope to collect information that is uniformly accurate.

ASKING THE QUESTIONS

You should avoid creating the impression that the interview is a quiz or cross-examination; be careful that nothing in your words or manner implies criticism, surprise, approval or disapproval either of the questions you ask or of the respondent's answers.

If you have a normal tone of voice, an attentive way of listening, and a nonjudgmental manner, you will maintain and increase the respondent's interest. Know the questions so well that you can read each one smoothly and move on to the next without any hesitancy. Study the questionnaire carefully and practice reading the questions aloud.

Ask the questions exactly as they are worded in the questionnaire. Since exactly the same questions must be asked of each respondent, you should not make changes in their phrasing. Avoid not only deliberate word changes, but also inadvertent ones. You may unwittingly leave out part of a question or change some of the words; or you may ask the question just as it is worded, but in an effort to be conversational, add a few words at the end of the question. For example, the questionnaire might read:

> "Where do you get most of your news about current events in this country — from the radio, the newspapers, TV, or talking to people?"

Now, consider the following variations on this wording:

> "Where do you get most of your news about current events?" (The last part of the question and the response categories are completely omitted.)

> "Where do you get most of your news about current events in this country — from the radio, the newspapers, or talking to people?" (One news source, TV, is omitted.)

> "Where do you get most of your news about current events in this country — from the radio, the newspapers, TV, or talking to people? That is, which one do you rely on most?" (Conversational comment added which changes the question completely.)

The respondent's answer is prompted by the words in the question, and a change in wording can very easily produce a change in response.

The above examples involve major changes in wording. Experiments show, however, that even a slight change in wording can distort results. For example, if the interviewer had merely changed the order in which she mentioned the news sources in the above question, it might have produced a bias. Research findings indicate that the order in which alternatives are presented can also affect responses. If the alternatives or fixed response categories are varied by some interviewers, the responses obtained cannot be combined accurately with the responses obtained by interviewers who adhere strictly to the original wording.

Read each question very slowly. Studies in interview methodology indicate that the ideal reading pace is two words per second. Even if you read a question correctly, it does not do much good if the words are all pushed together in a rush or lost in a mumble. A slow and deliberate pace gives the respondent time to understand the full scope of the question and to formulate a careful reply.

Interviewers may read too quickly for several reasons. Perhaps their natural rate of speaking is on the brisk side or perhaps the respondent has said "I only have half an hour so you'll have to hurry up!" The pell mell approach, far from speeding things up, may in fact tend to slow them down because so many questions have to be repeated. If the interviewer seems to hurry through the questions, there is a tendency for the respondent to hurry too; this may lead to an unfortunate pattern in which the interviewer asks the question before the respondent has quite finished the previous answer, and then the respondent starts the next answer before the interviewer has finished asking the question. Although you will become very familiar with the questionnaire during the course of a study, you must remember that it is all new to each respondent, and each should be given an equal chance to understand and respond to all of the questions.

Ask the questions in the order in which they are presented in the questionnaire. The question sequence is designed to create a sense of continuity and to ensure that early questions will not have a harmful effect on the respondent's answers to later questions. Furthermore, question order needs to be standardized from respondent to respondent if the interviews are to be comparable.

Ask every question specified in the questionnaire. In answering one question, a respondent will sometimes also answer another question which appears later in the interview. Or, from time to time, when the interviewer needs to ask a series of apparently similar questions, the respondent may ask, "Just put me down as 'Yes' to all of them." In these cases, you may wonder whether you should skip the questions which are apparently answered. You should not. *It is your responsibility to make certain, wherever possible, that the respondent is fully exposed to each question specified in the questionnaire.*

In the situation described above, you can use the following procedure: Write down the initial answer under the question when it occurs. Then ask the partially answered question when you get to it, but preface it with some remark which will show the respondent that you have not forgotten what he said earlier and have not rejected his earlier answer. You might say, for example: "We have already touched on this, but let me ask you . . ." or "We're asking people on this survey about each one of these, and I'd just like to make sure how you feel about each one separately. . . ." In those few cases in which the question has been clearly answered already, you might say, "You've told me something about this, but this next question asks . . ." For example:

Q: *Do you think you will be better off next year than you are now, or worse off, or what?*

A: We should be better off.

Q: *Why is that?*

A: I'm scheduled for a raise in salary on September 1.

Q: *Do you expect to be earning more money next year than you are now, or less, or what? You've already told me that you expect a raise . . . (expectant pause)*

A: Yes, but my wife will no longer be working, so actually we may earn just about the same amount of money, or even less. My son will have graduated from college though, and we won't have to support him, so we'll be better off (even though earning less money).

Assuming the respondent has already answered a question is a dangerous practice. Whenever possible, *ask every question,* even when it has been answered previously. Do this by letting the respondent know that you are aware of the earlier response, and asking the respondent's cooperation in answering again.

Repeat questions which are misunderstood or misinterpreted. Questions are phrased so that they will be understood by respondents all over the country, and you will find that most of the people you interview do indeed understand them. Occasionally, however, a respondent may misunderstand or misinterpret what is asked. When this happens, the best technique is to repeat the question just as it is written in the questionnaire. If you suspect that the respondent merely needs time to think it over, simply wait and do not press for an immediate answer. If you think the respondent just needs to be reassured, you may want to add a *neutral* conversational remark, such as: "We're just trying to get people's ideas on this," or "There are no right or wrong answers, just your ideas on it."

If the respondent asks for an explanation of a word or phrase, you should refrain from offering help and return the responsibility for the definition to the respondent. If, for example, the question asks, "Do you feel you personally have been discriminated against?" and the respondent inquires, "Do you mean discriminated against socially or in my job?" you should say something such as "Just whatever it means to you — anything *you* would call discrimination." If, however, the respondent does not know the meaning of the word "discrimination" and says, "I don't understand the question — what does it mean?" do not try to define or explain it but go on to the next question. In both cases, record the respondent's queries in the margin and indicate your replies in parentheses.

Keep track of changes you make in the questionnaire. Any changes — even inadvertent ones — that you make in the wording, phrasing, or order of questions in the interview should be noted in the questionnaire. This is necessary because study directors and coders must know what was asked in order to decide whether these altered questions can be used and how they should be coded.

Gathering personal data. Questions about the respondent's age, sex, schooling, marital status, income, religious preference, and so forth, are usually at the end of the questionnaire. At this point, the respondent will usually understand what is required and why it is important — he will also have learned to trust you and you should be able to obtain responses to these personal data questions with no resistance. If, however, the respondent asks why you want to know his age, religion, income, or other personal information, you might say something such as:

> "Well, as I was saying earlier, we are talking with people of different ages and various occupations in all parts of the country. We put all of the interviews together, and then count them up to see whether men feel differently from women, whether young people feel differently from older people, and so on. To do this we need to know a few things about the people we talk to. So, I have just a few questions on that type of thing."

These are logical reasons why we wish to have the information, and tell the respondent why his cooperation will be helpful. If there seems to be a need for further reassurance, you may add: "As I mentioned, the interview is completely confidential. The survey report is simply a summary of all the interviews, without, of course, identifying anyone." Occasionally, a respondent will feel strongly about telling you his income or his religion. In these cases, you should proceed to the next question without further probing.

If you are matter-of-fact in your approach, you probably will not encounter any problems. People are used to giving personal information to various agencies, and gathering data of this sort is much less difficult than new interviewers often imagine.

CLARIFYING THE RESPONDENT'S ROLE BY USING POSITIVE FEEDBACK

Since the respondent does not know ahead of time that he will be expected to fit his opinions into check boxes, think in terms of five and seven point scales, or take the temperature of his feelings by putting them on a paper thermometer, you must teach him the acceptable procedures as the interview progresses. Through a variety of signals, you can indicate to the respondent that he is doing a good job of answering the questions. This does *not* mean that you imply agreement or disagreement with his answers or attitudes, but rather that you approve of his behavior in his role as a respondent. This has nothing to do with how much he knows or how much you think he knows. Interviewers might think of a good respondent as one who is interesting and articulate, but for our purposes, a good respondent is one who learns and follows the conventions of a particular questionnaire.

It is admittedly discouraging for an interviewer to follow the correct interviewing techniques and still have the respondent say, "I just don't know anything about that at all," through a whole series of questions, or worse still, "I dunno" through a whole questionnaire. In the few instances in which this happens, interviewers feel they have failed in some way and often inquire if we will be able to use the interview because it contains little information. Of course, the interview can be used. The interviewer used proper techniques and the respondent was given the same stimulus as more knowledgeable respondents. To a social scientist, the fact that the respondent "didn't know" is valid information, even if it is not interesting for the interviewer.

Reinforce the respondent by giving him positive feedback in the form of neutral comments such as, "Yes," "OK," "I see," "Uh-huh," or even just a nod of the head, which indicate that you have heard and understood the response and that he is being a good respondent. At the same time, you must be careful not to give leading or unacceptable feedback or to reinforce bad behavior. For example, if the respondent says, "Gee, I can't decide — 70 seems too high and 60 seems too low," you should not try to be helpful and suggest 65 as a compromise, but should ask, "What number do you think might be closest to the way you feel?" The answers recorded in the questionnaire should reflect decisions made by the respondent, not by the interviewer.

Your social instincts may urge you to try to make the respondent feel comfortable in his role. This can backfire if it is used to reinforce bad or balky behavior. If the respondent seizes the offensive and says, "Nobody can answer *that* question — how should I know what business conditions will be like in five years?" and you, in an effort to smooth things over, say "Oh, that's all right, we'll just go on to the next question," you will encourage bad behavior by accepting it. Instead, repeat the question, preceded by a neutral comment such as, "Of course, no one knows for sure, but we're interested in people's opinions." Once the respondent realizes that it is your job to ask each question and his job to answer each one, the interview should proceed smoothly.

4 PROBING AND OTHER INTERVIEWING TECHNIQUES

One of the most challenging and important aspects of the interviewer's work is getting the respondent to answer the question which was asked. If your respondent gives you an incomplete or irrelevant answer, misunderstands the question, if you do not understand his answer, or if he loses track of the question and gets off on another topic, it is your responsibility to get him back on the track through careful, *neutral* techniques. The quality of the interview depends a great deal on the interviewer's ability to probe and use these techniques successfully.

Probing has two major functions:

- It motivates the respondent to communicate more fully so that he *enlarges* on, *clarifies,* or *explains the reasons* behind what he has said.
- It helps the respondent focus on the specific content of the interview so that irrelevant and unnecessary information can be avoided.

Probes must perform these two functions without introducing bias.

Obtaining specific, complete responses which satisfy the objectives of the questions can be the most difficult part of the interview. Some respondents have difficulty putting their thoughts into words; others may give unclear or incomplete answers; still others may be reluctant to reveal their attitudes because they feel that they are socially unacceptable. You must deal with such factors and use procedures which encourage and clarify responses.

Even the best questionnaire may elicit first responses which are inadequate. An answer may be inadequate because it is only a partial answer and therefore incomplete; it may also be irrelevant, about something other than the subject of the question, or it may be unclear. In the following examples, note how the inadequate replies fail to answer the question:

Q: *Do you think it will make a lot of difference to the country whether the Democrats or Republicans win the November elections, or that it won't make much difference which side wins?*

A: Yes, I do. (Unclear answer)

Q: *Considering the country as a whole, do you think we'll have good times, or bad times, or what, between now and a year from now?*

A: I hope we'll have good times. (Irrelevant answer)

The interviewer cannot accept these replies because they do not adequately fulfill the question objectives. Obviously, some method of returning the respondent's mind to the topic of the question is needed so that *clear, complete,* and *relevant* answers are obtained. This does not mean that the interviewer should openly question a respondent's answer, since the respondent probably thought he was answering the question correctly. Rather, by probing, the interviewer can encourage the respondent to clarify and expand his answer.

KINDS OF PROBES

Several different neutral techniques may be used to stimulate a fuller, clearer response.

Repeating the question. When the respondent does not seem to understand the question, when he misinterprets it, when he seems unable to make up his mind, or when he strays from the subject, the most useful technique is to repeat the question just as it is written in the questionnaire. Many respondents, hearing it for a second time, realize what kind of answer is needed. They may not have heard the question fully the first time, or they might have missed the question's emphasis. Often, further probes will then be unnecessary.

An expectant pause. The simplest way to convey to a respondent that you know he has begun to answer the question, but that you feel he has more to say, is to be silent. The pause — often accompanied by an expectant look or a nod of the head — gives the respondent time to gather his thoughts.

Accepting pauses during an interview is often difficult for the new interviewer. Sometimes you may have a desperate feeling that things must be kept moving, and a few seconds of silence seem to last forever. But pauses are often useful in encouraging communication, and they should become a natural part of your interviewing technique.

You must, however, be sensitive to each individual respondent in using pauses. Some respondents may actually be out of ideas, and a pause can become a yawning abyss rather than encouragement to further thought.

Repeating the respondent's reply. Simply repeating what the respondent has said as soon as he has stopped talking is often an excellent probe.

This should be done as you are writing, so that you are actually repeating the respondent's reply and recording it at the same time. Hearing his idea repeated often stimulates the respondent to further thought.

Neutral questions or comments. Neutral questions or comments are frequently used to obtain clearer and fuller responses. The following are examples of the most commonly used probes and their "key word" phrases or abbreviations which must be recorded in the questionnaire in parentheses:

Interviewer's Probe	Standard Abbreviation
Repeat question	(RQ)
Anything else?	(AE or Else?)
Any other reason?	(AO?)
Any others?	(Other?)
How do you mean?	(How mean?)
Could you tell me more about your thinking on that?	(Tell more)
Would you tell me what you have in mind?	(What in mind?)
What do you mean?	(What mean?)
Why do you feel that way?	(Why?)
Which would be closer to the way you feel?	(Which closer?)

These probes indicate that the interviewer is interested and they make a direct request for more information. This technique takes time to master, but it is a dependable and fruitful one when used correctly. New interviewers often find it useful to write these standard probes on a card and tape the card inside their interviewer's folder for easy reference.

Successful probing requires that you recognize immediately just how the respondent's answer has failed to meet the objective of the question and then be able to formulate a neutral probe to elicit the information needed. You know the question objectives; the respondent does not. It is your responsibility to study the instruction book thoroughly before starting to use the questionnaire. It is only through a complete understanding of the objectives that you can recognize when and where probes are needed and use them effectively. Your manner in asking these neutral questions is important. Of course, a strident, demanding tone of voice does not increase the respondent's desire to try again.

Instructions for a particular question or set of questions may indicate how forcefully the interviewer should probe. In these cases, remember that a longer sentence is likely to encourage more information than a short phrase. "Are there any other reasons why you feel that way?" gives the respondent time to think and lends importance to the request. "Any other?" is much more likely to elicit a "no" response.

Asking for further clarification. In probing, it will sometimes be useful for you to appear slightly bewildered by the respondent's answer and intimate with your probe that it might be you who failed to understand. For example: "I'm not quite sure I know what you mean by that — could you tell me a little more?" This technique can arouse the respondent's desire to cooperate with someone who he thinks is trying to do a good job. It should not be overplayed, however, or the respondent will get the feeling that you do not know when a question is properly answered.

NONDIRECTIVE PROBING

We have described probing as a technique that motivates a respondent to communicate more fully and that focuses his attention on specific topics. But probing must be done without introducing bias, and the potential for bias is great. Under pressure of the interviewing situation, an interviewer may imply quite unintentionally that some responses are more acceptable than others, or hint that a respondent might wish to consider or include this or that in giving a response.

Consider the question:

"How do you think things are going in the world today — I mean our relations with other countries?"

The respondent's first answer might be:

"Well, I don't know. In some ways they are going well and in some ways they are going poorly."

The respondent has not answered the question but has indicated some thoughts on the subject. How might the interviewer handle this situation? A neutral probe might be:

"I see; well, could you tell me what you have in mind?"

or

"There are no right or wrong answers on things like this, of course. I'd just like to get your thinking about it."

It is important not to change the content of the question. The following example illustrates a directive probe which violates this rule:

Probing and Other Interviewing Techniques

"Well, what about our relations with China?"

The respondent will then consider any answer in terms of our relations with China — a subject that neither the questionnaire nor the respondent had mentioned and that was introduced solely by the interviewer. It is not likely that the respondent would ever get back to what he really thought about "our relations with other countries."

The principle of nondirective probing does not apply in the same way when the question is asking for straight factual information. For example, if you are asking about total family income and your respondent seems to be considering only his own salary, it is perfectly acceptable to focus on the question by saying, "Does that include the income of your wife and children?" It is *not* acceptable to say, "You make more than $20,000, don't you?"

However, when asking attitudinal ("How do you feel about . . . ?") questions, you must be especially careful to use only neutral methods, because you can easily influence the respondent's expression of his attitude or opinion. Sometimes an answer may be suggested unconsciously by the inflection of your voice. Take the simple question:

"Do you think the United Nations is doing all it can to help keep peace in the world?"

Asked in a normal manner, this question prompts either a "Yes" or "No" answer. But the inflection of your voice can play all sorts of tricks with it. If you emphasize the word "all" you may get a higher than normal percentage of "No" responses. If you stress "United Nations," you are likely to get a high percentage of "Yes" answers.

Occasionally, a respondent will give an "I don't know" answer. This can mean any number of things. For instance:

- The respondent does not understand the question and answers "don't know" to avoid saying he does not understand.

- The respondent is thinking the question over and says "don't know" to fill the silence and to give himself time to think.

- The respondent may be trying to evade the issue, or he may feel that the question is too personal and does not want to hurt the interviewer's feelings by saying so in a direct manner.

- The respondent really may not know, or may not have an opinion or attitude on the subject.

If the respondent actually does not have the information which you request, this in itself is significant survey data. It is your responsibility to be sure that this is in fact the case, and not mistake "I have no opinion on that" for "Wait a minute, I'm thinking." A repetition of the question, an expectant pause, a reassuring remark ("Well, we're just interested in your general ideas about this.") or a neutral probe ("What are your ideas about this?") will all encourage the respondent to reply.

Since you know very little about your respondent's reaction to questions at the beginning of the interview, it is a good idea to probe all of the "don't know" responses that occur during the first few pages of a questionnaire. The most effective probing technique is to repeat the original question.

EXAMPLES OF PROBES

The primary question is:

"Considering the country as a whole, do you think we will have good times during the next year, or bad times, or what?"

Answer 1:

Yes, I do.

(What does the respondent mean? "Yes, we will have good times," and "Yes, we will have bad times," are both possible interpretations.)

Possible probes:

Let me make sure I understand you. Do you think we will have good times during the next year, bad times, or what?

Repeat answer, "You said yes . . ." (pause) . . . (repeat question).

What did you mean?

Answer 2:

I hope we have good times.

(This answer is irrelevant. The question asked what his expectations were, not what his wishes and hopes were.)

Possible probes:

We all hope we will have good times, but what do you *think* will happen?

Let me just read this question again . . . (repeat question).

Answer 3:

Well, we're all getting along better these days.

(This answer is irrelevant. The question asked for an expectation in absolute terms, not a statement of how things are now, or a relative answer comparing next year to this year.)

Possible probes:

I see, but would you say . . . (repeat question).

Yes, and thinking only about next year . . . (repeat alternatives emphasizing the words "*good* times" and "*bad* times").

Answer 4:

It will be good; my husband just got a promotion.

(This answer is irrelevant. The question asked about the country as a whole, not the respondent and her family.)

Possible probes:

That's nice, now . . . (repeat question, stressing the words "country as a whole").

Answer 5:

Maybe good, maybe bad. It all depends.

(The respondent may be saying that he just cannot tell, but he has not made that clear. Be careful not to misdirect the respondent by focusing on the word "depends".)

Possible probes:

What do you expect will happen?

Which would be closer to the way you feel? (Repeat alternatives.)

Can you tell me more about what you expect will happen?

5 RECORDING AND EDITING THE INTERVIEW

Even though you may do a good job of asking the questions and probing in order to meet the study objectives, the information which you gather will be lost if you cannot convey it to the coders in a full and unbiased form. Each interviewer must use the same format and conventions in transcribing the interview while it is being conducted and in editing each interview after it has been completed. You should record the respondent's replies as well as your own probes right in the questionnaire in the space provided for each question, so that each completed interview contains the original questions, your supplementary questions (probes) and comments, as well as the respondent's answers.

QUESTIONNAIRE FORMAT AND CONVENTIONS

The Center uses two basic types of questions in its questionnaires. These are:

- "Open-ended" questions — sometimes referred to as write-in or unrestricted questions.

- "Closed" questions — sometimes referred to as check-off or restricted questions.

There is a third type of question, the "write-up" or "in-depth" question which requires extensive probing. For this type of question, the interviewer takes notes on a separate pad and then writes up a full report immediately after the interview. It is used only for special studies by experienced interviewers especially trained in this technique.

The open-ended question. Open-ended questions are used when a full expression of opinion is desired. Surveys will often start off with open questions or use them in transitions to give respondents a chance to think about topics and express general feelings before they are asked about specific areas of a topic. Although closed questions are easier to code, it is impossible to frame questions about every conceivable aspect of a topic — for example, the quality of life in the United States today — so it is important to open it up and find out which areas of the topic are important to the respondent. For example:

Q1. Do you think there are some ways in which life in the United States is getting <u>worse</u>? (In what ways?)

_____

_____

Q2. Are there some ways in which you think life in the United States is getting <u>better</u>? (In what ways?)

_____

_____

Key words in the question are underlined, and the probe in parentheses is optional — to be used if the respondent just says "yes." The respondent's replies to these questions should be entered in the questionnaire, on the lines provided, during the interview and as the respondent is talking.

The closed question. In the closed question, the response categories are a part of the question and the interviewer checks the box containing the respondent's choice. The following is an example of a closed question which was asked immediately after the above open questions about life in the United States.

Q3. All things considered, do you think things are getting better, or worse, or that they are staying about the same, or what?

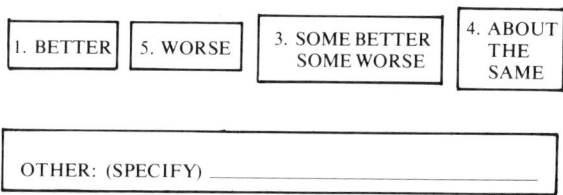

For this particular question, there is a provision for an "other" category outside the fixed responses in the boxes. There is also a "pro/con" category for people who do not want to commit themselves to "better" or "worse" and say instead, "Well, in some ways it's better and in some ways it's worse." The pro/con possibility is not read to the respondent, but a box is provided for the interviewer's convenience. For the next sample question, there is no provision in the questionnaire for an "other" response, but the closed question leads to an open-ended probe.

Q4. If you had a chance to move out of the United States and settle down for good in some other country, do you think you would like to do it?

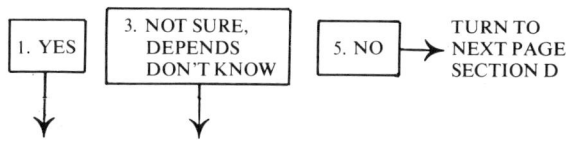

Q4a. What would be your main reason for wanting to move?

_____

_____

Each of the response choices leads either to a specific probe or to an interviewer instruction. The interviewer's eye travels to the probe or to the instruction because of the arrows from the response boxes.

Sometimes there will be a *choice* of terms or phrases to use in a question. You will know which choice to make either through observation or through previous questions. Whenever a wording choice occurs, the options will be set off in parentheses. For example:

A2. Are you (and your family) receiving as much income now as you were a year ago, or more, or less?

All of the interviewer instructions which should not be read to the respondent are printed in capital letters. Boxed response categories are usually printed this way, but if they appear in lower case, they should be read as part of the question. For example:

Q57. Does your (wife/husband) go to (church/synagogue) . . .

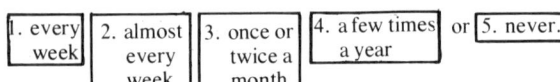

Because of the other demographic questions about religious preference which preceded this one, the interviewer would be able to pick out the appropriate option from the words shown in parentheses, then go on to read all of the response categories in the boxes.

In closed questions, the numbers in the boxes denote codes, so that you will be doing a form of coding when you put an "X" through the appropriate box.

RULES FOR RECORDING RESPONSES

A good written interview should record not only what the respondent said, but also the way in which he said it. It should relay the answers, and it should also transmit as accurately as possible a representation of the interview situation and of the respondent's personality. In order to accomplish this, you will need to follow a few rules for recording.

Record responses during the interview. In order to reproduce the responses accurately, you must write them down immediately during the interview. Relevant information will be lost or distorted if you try to remember what the respondent has said and write it up later.

Of course, you cannot let the respondent's attention wander while you write laboriously in the questionnaire. It is possible, with patience and concentration, to enter full notes in the questionnaire while the respondent is talking.

Use the respondent's own words. You must learn to record the respondent's replies in the very words which he uses. This is called "verbatim reporting." Try to note the phrases, grammatical usage, and peculiarities of speech which are characteristic of each respondent, so that the interview will reflect something of his individual personality. This will give the interview color and animation. Do not attempt to record dialect, but do mention it in your thumbnail sketch at the end of the interview.

Do not summarize or paraphrase the respondent's answers. Summarizing or paraphrasing a response creates an artificial and dangerous communication gap between the respondent and the data analyst, and often results in distortion. Consider the difference between the following examples.

Verbatim recording:

I am very upset about the Middle East and I have been for years. The Palestinian refugees have been a desperate problem but no one paid any attention until the Arabs pulled the plug in the oil tank.

Summarized version:

Problems in Middle East — Arabs, oil, etc.

The summarized recording lacks the intensity and luster of the respondent's reply, but the problem is much more serious than this. The paraphrased answer actually distorts the meaning of the respondent's reply. The specific references which the respondent makes, the words he uses, the examples he gives, the length of his answer, all provide important information.

The above example is rather extreme. Consider now the much more subtle change of emphasis in the following example.

Verbatim recording:

Yes, indeed! I certainly do think so.

Summarized version:

Yes.

Include everything that pertains to the question objectives. The recorded response should include everything the respondent said that pertains to the objectives of the question, regardless of length. Some respondents will digress from the topic and talk at length about subjects that have no bearing on the study objectives. Long irrelevant discourses may be omitted from the recorded interview IF:

• You are certain that what is being said has no bearing on or use in fulfilling the aims of the study.

• You make marginal notes to indicate that a digression took place.

You may summarize a true digression by entering your own comment in the margin of the questionnaire, right where the digression occurred in the interview. Such explanatory notes should always appear in parentheses. For example:

(Here R talked at length about his son's war experiences.)

or

(R talked about problems she is having with her teenage daughter.)

Include all of your probes. All comments, probes, and explanations which you make during the course of the interview *should appear in the questionnaire at the location which corresponds to the point at which they were made during the interview.* By examining these, the coders and analysts can determine what influenced the respondent to reply as he did. Always enter probes and comments in parentheses.

Hold the respondent's interest. Try to keep your attention focused on the respondent, and not to become overly absorbed in the questionnaire. A good technique for holding the respondent's interest *and* taking verbatim notes is to start repeating the response, *as you are writing it down.* This lets the respondent know you are listening to every word — and, in fact, recording each one. And, as we pointed out previously, this technique also serves as a "probe." The respondent will hear what he has just said, and this may stimulate further thought and lead him to amplify or modify his statement. An example of this technique follows:

Q: *What would you say are the main differences between schools nowadays compared with what they were like when you went to school?*

A: Schools are far more advanced right from the start — in the second and third grades they teach them more than we had at those grades.

Q: (*as* you are writing the last few words of the reply) . . . *they teach them more than we had at those grades.* (Pause)

A: Yes. You know — nowadays they teach languages even in grade school.

It will help you to *start recording as soon as the respondent starts talking* rather than to look at the respondent all the time he is replying. Occasional eye contact is important, however, and you should glance up now and then, especially when you are *asking* the questions.

TIPS ON NOTE TAKING

With practice you will be able to record your interviews with little difficulty. Try recording part of a radio newscast, practice on a friend, etc. The following tips can help you become adept at speedy recording.

When starting the interview, try to find a place where you will be able to write comfortably. A dining room or kitchen table is ideal, but just in case a table is not available, always carry a folder or pad that you can use for a hard writing surface. Your blue University of Michigan folder will serve this purpose very well. Try to sit so that you are facing the respondent and avoid being in a position which allows the respondent to look over your shoulder as you write.

When the respondent starts to talk, begin to write immediately. This will help you record the responses verbatim and minimize the time the respondent has to wait for the next question. Most questionnaires are printed with plenty of room for responses and marginal comments, but you should always carry a pad with you just in case you need extra writing space. A lengthy answer may be recorded on a separate sheet of paper as long as the paper is properly identified as belonging to a particular interview and a particular question.

In addition to the probing abbreviations on page 16, use the following standard abbreviations to help you record faster:

R ....respondent
I'er ....interviewer
I'w ....interview
I'ing ....interviewing
DK ....don't know
(RQ) ....repeated (survey) question
T'nail ....Thumbnail Sketch
Q'naire ....questionnaire
Inap ....question is inappropriate by study definition

Abbreviate sentences. You can do this by leaving out articles and prepositions, by entering only key words, and so on. Then later, while you are editing the interview, put these in along with punctuation so that the coders can read the responses as they were actually given.

In the case of standard probes all you need to do is write the two or three key words of the probe in parentheses. For instance, (How mean?) is all you need to write to show you used the standard probe, "How do you mean?" and (What mind?) would show you used "Will you tell me what you have in mind?" Any nonstandard probe must be written out in full.

MECHANICS OF RECORDING AND EDITING INTERVIEWS

The Center requires a uniform procedure for recording interviews. It will be easier for you as well as for the coder and the analyst if you follow these procedures:

Use a pencil to record. Please use a number 2 black lead pencil to record the respondent's answers; a harder lead keeps its point longer, but gives a faint impression and is difficult for the coder to read. *Do not use a pen.* Carry several pencils with you so that you will always have a sharp one.

In jotting down key words and phrases you may leave out small words such as "and," "I," and "the," and abbreviate longer words. After the interview, you must then edit your recordings so that the responses are clear. You may erase and rewrite illegible words, but you must never substitute your own words for the respondent's or try to tidy up the grammar. Please do *not* erase any calculations you may have made in the margin as it is often useful to know how you and the respondent arrived at figures for rent, income, days of vacation, etc.

Writing must be legible. Regardless of how good the actual interview may have been, it will be worthless if your record of it is unreadable. When you edit an interview, please check to be sure that all of your writing is legible.

Use parentheses to indicate the interviewer's words or observations. Parentheses should be used to distinguish clearly between the respondent's words and anything you say or do.

Parentheses should be used for the following items:

- All probes you use in the interview.
- All remarks and explanations you make to the respondent.
- Comments you wish to make to the coders and analysts, such as:
  —descriptions of respondent behavior;
  —summaries of respondent digressions;
  —cross references and marginal notes;
  —reason(s) why a question was not asked.

Do not put anything the respondent says in parentheses. We assume that anything *not* in parentheses is in the respondent's own words, so that it is not necessary to use quotation marks. Please make sure that any incomplete verbatim answer will make sense to the coder by including explanatory notes in the margin.

Cross reference relevant material in the interview. During editing, you should cross reference the responses to one question that also apply to other questions. This will tell the coder to read other relevant information.

A respondent may think of something he would like to add to an earlier response, or he may give you some information after the interview is completed. Again, record the information on the questionnaire at the point which corresponds to the point at which it was given to you in the interview. Then, when you are editing, enter a cross reference in the proper places so that the coders will easily find all of the relevant information. Such a cross reference might read:

Q4. (See Q10.)   or   Q4. (See t'nail.)

Please enter cross references in parentheses in the questionnaire to distinguish them clearly from anything the respondent says.

Account for each question in the questionnaire. You must either record an answer for each question or explain why it was not answered. Please make sure *every* unanswered question has some explanation with it. The Center has standard abbreviations for unasked questions as follows:

(*Inap*)   This is the abbreviation for *inapplicable* or *inappropriate,* and should be used only when the questionnaire instructs the interviewer to skip questions because of the

Recording and Editing the Interview

respondent's earlier answers. You should never mark a question (Inap) because *you feel* it is inappropriate, but only when the questionnaire instructions say it is.

A slashmark may be drawn across an entire page, or across a group of questions on a page in place of or in conjunction with the abbreviation (Inap).

(Skipped) If a question is skipped either intentionally or accidentally, write *Skipped* in the margin and always give an explanation.

With the exception of the abbreviation "DK" (don't know), please do not use words on the lines for answers requiring dollar amounts. A zero (0) should be used only for those questions calling for answers in dollar amounts and when the response is "none" or "no" or "not any" or some other equivalent of zero. A zero should *not* be used if the question was not asked.

Illustration 5-1, the facsimile of a page from a questionnaire, shows how some of these abbreviations and symbols are used in recording an interview. When the respondent answered "No" to question H9, the interviewer put an "X" in the "no" response category box. This will then be coded "5." Please put the "X" across the word in the box and not across the number. Note that the interviewer circled the sources of income mentioned by the respondent in H11. This does not change the code category, but it clarifies the information.

If you find that you have checked the wrong response category, erase the incorrect mark and check the correct box. If the respondent changes his mind, please leave the original mark in the questionnaire, draw an arrow to the new response category, and make a marginal note.

G5. How often do you think the police treat teenagers fairly in your (community)? Do you think they are often treated fairly, sometimes treated fairly, or never treated fairly?

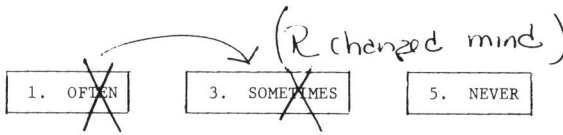

Identify each interview. Center interviews require certain basic identification such as your name, the date, your interview number, PSU, etc. This information should appear on the cover sheet for each interview as well as on the questionnaire. Such identification is necessary for Center use only; it is never used to identify a respondent. *Include the following information in the upper right-hand corner on any additional write-up sheets that may accompany the interview:*

- Interviewer's name
- Project number
- Your interview number
- Date interview was taken
- PSU name

THE THUMBNAIL SKETCH

A space is provided at the end of the questionnaire for you to enter a short description of the respondent and the interview situation. This is a good place to capture the special flavor of the respondent or the situation. You can also "blow off steam" here about the interview. Coders turn first to the thumbnail sketch so that they can get some idea about the personality behind the responses before they start translating these responses into numbers.

A thumbnail sketch could contain the following type of information:

- The respondent's attitude and his family's attitude toward you and the survey.
- Unusual circumstances and events that had any bearing on the interview such as interruptions, language difficulty, etc.
- Feelings that you might have about the respondent and the interview, things you sense or suspect.
- Anything else that happened while you were at the respondent's home that has any bearing on the survey objectives.

A good rule of thumb(nail) is to include in your sketch any information that would enable you to recall this particular respondent and/or the interview situation. "Good interview, no problems" is not very revealing.

Remember that respondents have a legal right to come to Ann Arbor and ask to look at their interviews — including the comments in the thumbnail sketch. "R had trouble with the cards, also limited interest in the survey compounded by three small, demanding children," is an appropriate comment to put in the thumbnail — "This was the dumbest R I have ever interviewed" is not.

Please do not enter any action requests or ask the office any questions in the thumbnail! The Field Office personnel, unlike coders and analysts, do *not* usually read the thumbnail, so that your requests or questions could be overlooked.

Illustration 5-1
EXAMPLE OF COMPLETED QUESTIONNAIRE PAGE

H9. In addition to this, did you have any income from bonuses, overtime, or commissions?

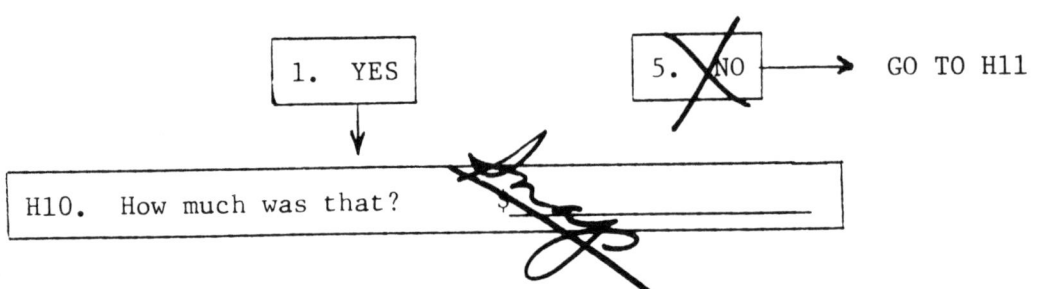

1. YES

5. ~~NO~~ → GO TO H11

H10. How much was that? ~~~~

H11. Did you (HEAD) receive any other income in 1972 from:

IF "YES" TO ANY ITEM, ASK "How much was it?" ENTER AMOUNT & WEEK/MO/YR

IF "NO" ENTER "0"

a) professional practice or trade? $ 0 per ____
b) farming or market gardening, roomers or boarders? $ 0 per ____
c) dividends, (interest), rent, trust funds, or royalties? $ 300 per year
d) ADC, AFDC? $ 0 per ____
e) other welfare? $ 0 per ____
f) Social Security? $ 0 per ____
g) other retirement pay, (pensions), or annuities? $ 50 per month
*h) (unemployment), or workmen's compensation? $ 350 per *
i) alimony? Child support? $ 0 per ____
j) help from relatives? $ 0 per ____
k) anything else? won the lottery $ 50 per just w
   (SPECIFY)   once in

*h) unemployment $50 per week for 7 weeks
  50
 × 7
 ───
 $350

H12. Did anyone (else) not living here now help you (FAMILY) out financially-- I mean give you money, or help with your expenses during 1972?

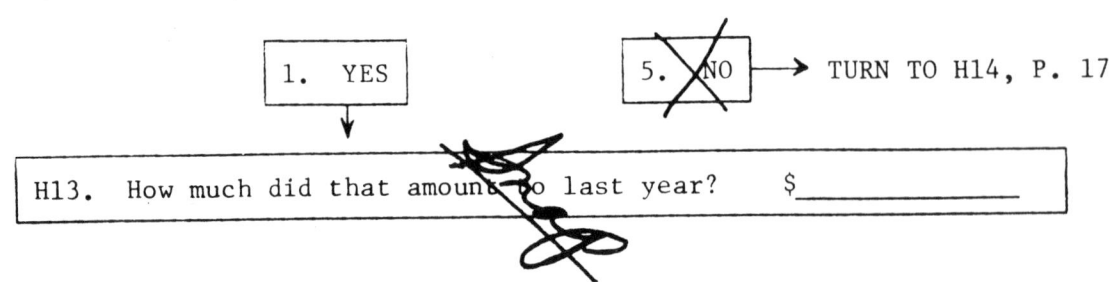

1. YES

5. ~~NO~~ → TURN TO H14, P. 17

H13. How much did that amount to last year? $ ~~~~

SUMMARY TIPS ON EDITING

When you edit, please remember that someone who was not present when you took the interview will be examining it. Even if you have asked a question, probed, and obtained a full answer, the entire response can be lost if the coder cannot understand what you wrote.

The best time to edit an interview is right after you take it, when the entire situation is still clear. Sometimes it is not possible to edit immediately, but try not to let more than a day elapse between the interview and the editing. Please be sure that:

• All entries are legible. As was mentioned earlier, the best response is worthless if it cannot be read.

• Inappropriate questions are clearly marked "Inap." Make sure the questions you mark "Inap" are really inappropriate according to the questionnaire instructions and not inadvertent omissions.

• All probes, and any other of your remarks during the interview, are indicated in parentheses.

• All unclear responses are clarified by your parenthetical notes.

• You have provided a full thumbnail sketch. This will give the reader a good idea of the interviewing situation and will help close the gap between the actual interview and the interview analysis.

After you have edited the interview, you should also carefully go over the cover sheet. Here are some suggestions for editing the cover sheet:

• Check to see that all necessary identification is on each cover sheet — your interviewer's name label, your interview number, the date, the length of the interview in minutes, your PSU name, segment number, line number, and the complete specific address of the HU.

• Make sure the specific address appears on the cover sheet in exactly the same words as it appears on the listing sheet.

• Complete the call record.

• Complete the nonresponse boxes on the back of the cover sheet for any address at which you are unable to obtain an interview. Provide as much information as possible for any noninterview situations.

EXAMPLES OF RECORDED RESPONSES

Examine Illustrations 5-2 and 5-3, which are other examples of completed questionnaire pages. Try to identify:

• A probe entry.

• An abbreviation of "repeated survey questions."

• A cross reference.

• A marginal note for a respondent digression.

• A respondent's side comments that explain the checked box.

• Clearly marked boxes.

TAPE RECORDING INTERVIEWS

There is another kind of "recording" which plays an important part in interviewing: tape recording. Interviewers are frequently asked to record their interviews, and the tapes are then used to evaluate both the interviewing technique and the adequacy of the questions. Tape recorders are used extensively in the training, retraining, and self-evaluation of interviewers.

General instructions. If you have never used a tape recorder before, you should first become completely familiar with its mechanics. (See the instructions which accompany the machine.) Use it for a practice interview, play it back, and try it again if you are not satisfied. If you feel comfortable using the machine, your respondents will too.

Be sure the machine is working properly *before* you leave home to interview. If you are using a cadmium battery pack, be sure it is fully charged. If you are using flashlight batteries, be sure they are fresh and *always* carry the electric power cord for your machine "just in case . . ."

Always ask the respondent for permission to record the interview. "I would like to tape this interview if that is all right," or "The University has asked me to tape these interviews if that is agreeable to you," are appropriate ways of introducing the subject. You may also explain that it helps you to make sure you have recorded the respondent's views accurately. We have used tape recordings for years in all parts of the country and respondents seldom refuse these requests. Most respondents do not know what to expect in an interview situation — the interviewer sets the rules, and if you use a tape recorder, then the respondent will assume that it is a natural part of the procedure.

Put the machine on the table between you and the respondent; you or your supervisor or the

Illustration 5-2
EXAMPLE OF COMPLETED QUESTIONNAIRE PAGE

A1. We are interested in how people are getting along financially these days. Would you say that you (and your family) are <u>better off</u> or <u>worse off</u> financially than you were <u>a year ago</u>?

| 1. BETTER NOW | 3. ~~SAME~~ | 5. WORSE NOW | 8. DON'T KNOW |

A1a. Why do you say so? Both of us got raises this year but we're just holding our own against inflation

(IF NOT ALREADY ANSWERED)

A2. Are you (and your family) receiving as much income now as you were a year ago, or more, or less?

| 1. ~~MORE NOW~~ | 3. ABOUT THE SAME | 5. LESS NOW |

I just told you! (See A1a)

A3. Now looking ahead--do you think that <u>a year from now</u> you (and your family) will be <u>better off</u> financially, or <u>worse off</u>, or just about the same as now?

Well

| 1. ~~WILL BE BETTER OFF~~ | 3. SAME | 5. WILL BE WORSE OFF | 8. DON'T KNOW |

but if the inflation keeps on it won't help much.

A4. Now turning to business conditions in the country as a whole--do you think that during the next 12 months we'll have <u>good times</u> financially, or <u>bad</u> times, or what? Of course I hope we'll have good times (yes, but what think?) Well I'd say

1. GOOD TIMES	4. BAD WITH QUALIFICATIONS
2. GOOD WITH QUALIFICATIONS	5. ~~BAD TIMES~~
3. PRO-CON	8. DON'T KNOW → TURN TO P.2, A5

A4a. Why do you think that? Gas just went up 10¢ a gallon- we have three cars and five drivers. (RQ-country as a whole?) There's the whole oil mess and the economy is so dependent on the auto industry

(R talks at length about house in country, kids in school, car pools, etc.)

Illustration 5-3
EXAMPLE OF COMPLETED QUESTIONNAIRE PAGE

(CARD C2, ORANGE) Some people are primarily concerned with doing everything possible to protect the legal rights of those accused of committing crimes. Others feel that it is more important to stop criminal activity even at the risk of reducing the rights of the accused.

Throw them all in jail! (RQ- What # on scale shows how feel?)

```
Protect Rights                                Stop Crime
 of Accused                                   Regardless of
                                              Rights of Accused
     ↓                                              ↓
|----|----|----|----|----|----|----|
     1    2    3    4    5    6    7
```

(INTERVIEWER RECORD NUMBER)

C2a. Where would you place yourself on this scale, or haven't you thought much about this?   a. __4__

0. HAVEN'T THOUGHT MUCH		8. DK
↓		
TURN TO P. 10, C3		

C2b. Where would you place most policemen?   b. __6 or 7__ (which closest)

I don't know any policemen (what think? most policemen)

| 8. DK |

C2c. Where would you place most people who have gone to college? *My generation or now? (most people)*   c. __2__

| 8. DK |

C2d. Where would you place most people who have not gone to college?   d. __—__

| 8. ✗ DK | *(R didn't want to be grouped)*

C2e. Where would you place most people about your age?   e. __4__

| 8. DK | *About where I am*

C2f. Where would you place most people your parents' age?   f. __6__

| 8. DK | *They're all squares (where place on scale?)*

(I had to keep reminding R about the scale.)

Field Office staff need to hear *both* you and the respondent. If possible, put the machine on a magazine or folded newspaper; this will help absorb some of the motor noise produced by vibration against a bare table top.

If you are using an external microphone, be sure that the mike is turned to "ON" and left on. Do not let the respondent hold the mike or fiddle with the "ON/OFF" button.

Use 90-minute cassette tapes. The shorter ones are not adequate for a whole interview, and the longer ones tend to become tangled. These tapes will usually be supplied to you when taping is requested. If you have to buy them, enter the cost on your expense voucher so that you will be reimbursed. Do not try to find bargains in tapes; usually they produce bargain quality recordings.

Since each side of the cassette records for 45 minutes, it is a good idea to put a note to yourself in the questionnaire at a convenient place to turn the tape. Do not bother to rewind to the beginning of side 2; just start right off and remember when you listen to the tape that there will be some blank tape at the beginning of side 2. Except when you turn the tape, please do not turn the machine on and off during the course of the interview unless there are lengthy interruptions.

You must *write* the responses, comments, and probes onto the questionnaire just as you would if the tape recorder were not there. The time you decide not to bother and try to write it up from the tape will be the time the machine does not work or the time a respondent's toddler turns off the mike while you are not looking.

Editing tape recorded interviews. The same rules of editing outlined earlier in this chapter apply whether or not the interview is tape recorded. You should edit the interview as soon as possible, making sure the correct boxes are checked, and that all relevant responses, probes, and so forth are written legibly into the questionnaire. Generally, it is not a good idea to try to do the complete editing job from the tape, as this is unnecessarily time-consuming. If a response is not clear, you may wish to refresh your memory by listening to that part of the tape.

Evaluation of your interviewing technique. After you have edited the interview, you should listen to the tape and "observe" your interviewing technique. Did you read all the questions exactly as worded? Did you probe where necessary? Did you make sure that the objectives of the questions were met? Did you read slowly and clearly, giving your respondent time for a considered reply? Was your approach to the respondent professional, showing neither approval nor disapproval, but rewarding him positively for his performance rather than for his responses?

A tape recording can give you valuable insight into your own performance as an interviewer. It is very difficult to evaluate your performance when you are in the midst of an interview, and the tape, in effect, gives you a chance to observe yourself.

Appendix D in this manual contains the code which will be used by your supervisor in evaluating your tapes. The criteria for interviewer behavior shown in this code are useful guidelines and standards for all interviewing, whether or not you use a tape recorder. Do *not* tape record telephone interviews.

6 CALL AND CALLBACK STRATEGY

Every sample address on a study must be accounted for with a cover sheet. We must account for dwellings which are unoccupied or which contain no eligible respondent as well as for those in which there is a person to be interviewed. Since you will not always find the respondent at home on the first call, callbacks are often necessary.

SUGGESTED PROCEDURES

The manner in which you make initial calls and subsequent callbacks can greatly affect response rates and costs. Please use the following suggestions as a guide.

- **Make calls at all of the assigned housing units early in the study period.** This will get you off to a good start and will allow you time to make repeated callbacks for respondents who are difficult to reach.

- **Plan trips to maximize the number of calls per trip.**

- **Plan to do your work in large blocks of time,** especially during the early part of the study.

- **Plan trips in accordance with your knowledge of the typical routines of people in your areas** and the changes in these routines from season to season. For example, in rural areas, people tend to be at home before 4 p.m. more often than they are in urban areas. Weekends may be a good time to find people at home in the late fall, but a poor time in the late spring. Depending on the area, you may have to plan your work around weekend sailing regattas or the deer hunting season.

Good times to call will also vary with respondent selection. For example, if the selected respondent is the head of a household in an urban or suburban area, it would probably be best to call in the late afternoon, early evening, or on a weekend when he is most likely to be home. However, a farmer might be delighted to see you at 10 o'clock on a winter morning.

- **It is best to start working at the beginning of the study in areas in which people are hardest to contact,** but you should not neglect segments on the way to or from the difficult area. Also start early in areas which are most apt to be affected by adverse weather conditions during the study; consider spring floods, snow which might close the mountain pass into a remote area, etc.

- **If no one is at home when you first call, try to get an idea of when someone is likely to be there** and note this on the cover sheet. If you cannot get any information, call at different times of the day, on different days of the week and on weekends. Because you will be talking to many people and keeping track of many schedules, you will find the call record on the cover sheet very useful in planning times to call. Not only is the call record helpful for the current study; it may also be of considerable help to you or another interviewer trying to locate this respondent for a reinterview on a future study. Often you can find out when a potential respondent is likely to be at home just by asking his neighbors. Plan to make one call in each of three distinct time periods:

1) *Days* during the week (9 a.m. to 6 p.m.)
2) *Evenings* during the week (6 p.m. or later)
3) *Weekends.*

- **Use discretion in setting up a definite appointment for an interview.**

  — If you do make an appointment, try to make it at the beginning of your day's trip so that you can make other calls after the interview and so that you will not find yourself in the middle of an interview when you should be keeping another appointment.

  — Good times for appointments are often the times that are bad for making initial calls, e.g., early in the morning or during the lunch hour. Try not to set up appointments during hours which are most productive for initial calls.

  — Be prepared to do other work during odd time periods between appointments when there is too little time to conduct another interview. This might include editing interviews, completing progress reports, or corresponding with your supervisor and the Field Office. Many interviewers travel with a tidy "office" in the trunk of their cars and some of the best thumbnail sketches have been written by interviewers waiting for an elusive respondent.

  — If a respondent breaks an appointment (or two), try stopping by, unannounced, when you are in the neighborhood.

  — Do not use the telephone for initial contacts on household surveys; it is too easy for a respondent to refuse an interview.

But you may certainly use the telephone to confirm an appointment if the respondent suggests it.

— Sometimes just one segment has been selected in an out-of-the-way place. The most efficient way to handle this kind of assignment is to pick an optimum time for the first visit to the area and try to set up appointments at all the assigned HU's at that time. By all means, call to confirm these appointments before you drive half way across the county.

• **Use the interviewer card for personal notes,** such as "Sorry I missed you . . ." when you are unable to find anyone at home. If the appointment was broken and you feel that the respondent is cooperative but absent-minded, you might leave your telephone number and ask him to call you to arrange a convenient time, adding something like "I will be back in your neighborhood Thursday and Friday . . ."

• **Drive by sites of future interviews.** As you go to and from interviews in the neighborhood, drive by a selected house even if you do not have time to stop and call. You may get clues as to when respondents are likely to be home (a car in the driveway) that will help you plan future calls.

• **Occasionally you may have a segment for which you feel the best strategy is a "blitz"** because the houses are close together and the neighbors do a lot of visiting among themselves. In such cases, and particularly if the interview is long, it may be best to have several interviewers working in the segment at the same time to clean it up as rapidly as possible.

• **If you have an "albatross" segment** where you have never had much luck, it may help your morale if you plan to work this segment along with your "lucky" segment where it is always a pleasure to interview.

RELUCTANT RESPONDENTS

Sometimes in spite of your best efforts a respondent will politely (or impolitely) refuse to be interviewed. Although experience will help you avoid refusals and minimize your disappointment when you get one, the following suggestions may be helpful.

• **Leave the door open for another try at a later time.** If you find you are not getting anywhere at all during your first meeting with the respondent, try to leave before you get a final "no" and before he starts to think of you as a pest. It may just be a bad time for him, he may have had an argument with his boss, or any number of other problems may be bothering him. Call back some other day when he might be in a better mood. Make an appointment to return if he suggests one, but remember that if he really wants to avoid the interview, he will know when to avoid being there.

• **Try not to let another member of the household refuse for the selected respondent.** "My husband certainly wouldn't be interested in anything like that!" Be particularly dubious about such statements if a wife has just said that she *would* be willing to be interviewed. If you get a refusal from the spouse of a respondent, diplomatically explain that while they might be correct in their assessment of your chances for the interview, your job requires that you talk to the selected respondent in person. In order to avoid such refusals, make the initial call at a time when you are most likely to find the selected respondent at home.

• **Try a persuasion letter.** If you feel that a personal letter from the Center might reverse a refusal or be reassuring to a reluctant respondent, please write the Field Office on an Immediate Action Memo and request that a persuasion letter be sent. These letters are essentially form letters, but they can be tailored to suit the circumstances. Information which should be included in your request:

— *Mailing address* (including the ZIP code) plus the segment and line number.
— *The person to whom the letter should be sent* (identify by relationship to head or by name if appropriate and available). If the person to whom the letter should be sent is the head of a household, be sure to indicate that person's sex so that we will know whether to use "Dear Sir" or "Dear Madam."
— *Circumstances of refusal.* Let us know if some person in the household kept you from interviewing the selected respondent or if the respondent refused to be interviewed and why.
— *The name of the interviewer.* The letter will give your name as the person who made the initial call. Please let us know if you or another interviewer will be calling back after the respondent has received the letter and we will mention this at the end of the letter.

Persuasion letters often convince respondents

that we really do mean what we tell them and that we really do want to talk with them.

• **In primary areas with more than one interviewer working on the study, ask the FC to assign the cover sheet to another interviewer.** If you do not seem to be getting any closer to an interview with a prospective respondent, perhaps another interviewer might be more successful. Again, try to avoid a definitive "no" so that another interviewer can try either with or without a persuasion letter.

Refusals are a source of concern to organizations such as the Center because they introduce bias into the survey findings. The Center studies nonresponse situations in an effort to determine the reasons behind them, better ways of avoiding them, and the degree of bias they introduce into the survey results. For these reasons, please give as much information as you can about nonresponse situations, especially refusals. Any demographic data on the noninterview respondent — age, sex, marital status, number of children, type of dwelling, and so on — are helpful.

The following is a list of ways in which a respondent might express his refusal.

- No reason given — respondent gives a flat "no" or "not interested" type of answer.
- Respondent expresses anti-government, anti-administration, anti-business, etc., feelings.
- Respondent expresses the feeling that surveys are "silly" or "not worthwhile."
- Respondent speaks a foreign language and is suspicious of your mission.
- Respondent seems antagonistic toward you but has no real reason for not wanting to be interviewed.
- Respondent says he is "too busy."
- Respondent says he is working and can not or does not want to take time for the interview.
- Respondent was previously interviewed by some other survey or sales organization which misrepresented the reason for the visit.

There may also be unexpressed reasons behind a respondent's refusal to grant an interview such as:

- The respondent feels personally threatened in some way by the interview or worried because he feels he does not know enough about the topic of the survey.
- The respondent may not believe that your real purpose is to conduct an interview.
- The respondent does not clearly understand the purpose of the study or why he is being asked to participate.

7 TELEPHONE INTERVIEWING (REINTERVIEWING)

We use the telephone for reinterviews in order to save both time and money. By reinterviewing our national cross-section sample, we can effectively measure changes in opinion over a time span of three, six, or nine months. It takes about two weeks to reinterview a cross section by telephone and costs about one-fifth as much as it would to conduct personal interviews.

TELEPHONE INTERVIEWING TECHNIQUES

In order to read the questions exactly, probe, and record telephone responses verbatim, simply employ the same techniques described for personal interviewing. Because you will not have any eye contact and you will have fewer intuitive clues as to whether or not the respondent understands the questions, it is even more important to read the questions slowly and clearly. It is also essential to edit the interview as soon as it is completed.

Although most of the time you will be reinterviewing respondents you have interviewed before, we do not feel it is practical or economical for one interviewer to work on an assignment which involves fewer than 10 cover sheets. Therefore, in some primary areas with relatively small sample sizes, one interviewer may conduct all of the telephone reinterviews for one study.

Since the first interviewer will already have established a rapport with the respondents, and since they will be familiar with the interviewing process, it should not be a problem for another interviewer to conduct the reinterviews if the introductory statement is clear. Introduce yourself as a representative of the Survey Research Center of The University of Michigan, and describe the study briefly, emphasizing that the reinterview will be much shorter than the original interview. If you did not conduct the first interview, mention the original interviewer's name and the date of the previous interview or interviews. You will have the telephone recontact sheet from the personal interview showing the respondent's name and relationship to the head of the household. Be sure you are reinterviewing the same respondent!

Also be sure that you have set aside enough time to conduct the interview when you place your call. You may find that you need to make appointments with your family as well as with your respondents, especially if you have teenaged children at home.

If the respondent seems reluctant to talk when you call, offer to call back at a more convenient time. Most reinterviews take about 30 minutes, and it is best to catch the respondent when he has sufficient time available. It is important to reassure him that the reinterview will be much shorter than the original interview, and that it will make his original effort even more valuable to our study.

Because some respondents will remember the previous interview clearly, they may sometimes respond with "I told you that before" or "the same as before." Do not accept such answers. We are attempting to measure *changes* in people's attitudes and expectations, and answers such as these tend to hide any changes that might have occurred. Many respondents change their attitudes without realizing it. If a respondent asks why it is necessary for us to ask questions similar to those he has already answered in the earlier survey, tell him that some respondents will have changed their circumstances or their opinions even if he has not. Be careful not to imply that the respondent should try to remember what he said before, or to remember whether his own attitudes or circumstances have changed.

Recording and editing. In telephone interviews, there will be long silences while you write down what the respondent says. One way to fill those silences is to explain that you are pausing to write. You might utter an occasional "umm-umm" as you write, or you may repeat the answer as you write, just as you would do in a personal interview. For questions that do not have boxes to check, it is perfectly acceptable to underline parts of the question which correspond to the respondent's answer.

In a telephone survey it is especially important that you edit your interviews *immediately* after you hang up, to be sure that all responses are complete and legible. As always, you should take time to record the respondent's answers as completely as possible, but that will not help us if we cannot read what you have written. Since both the interviewing and the coding period are very short, there is no opportunity to ask an interviewer to clarify missing or garbled information. Such information must be coded "NA" (Not Ascertained).

Since telephone studies usually have a short interviewing period (two weeks) and an inflexible deadline, you must start calling your respondents as soon as you have received your materials and studied the instructions. Practice interviews are not usually required, but it is a good idea to read the questionnaire aloud before you start production interviewing. Calls should be made in the evenings as well as in the mornings and afternoons. If at first you do not succeed, try different hours of the day and different days of the week. Please do not tape record telephone interviews, either with or without the respondent's permission.

8 SAMPLING PRINCIPLES AND PROCEDURES

Survey sampling is the process of selecting certain members of a group in such a way that they will represent the total group about which we wish to make generalized statements. The selection process is extremely important; no matter how good the interviews are, the results of our surveys will not be accurate if the respondents have been selected improperly.

Accurate sampling requires a combination of sound planning in the office and careful execution by interviewers in the field. Most of SRC's studies, especially large nationwide surveys, involve interviewing one member of a household. The following chapters on sampling will discuss procedures for selecting households and individuals to be interviewed. The same principles could also be applied to surveys which are not nationwide, although the specific procedures might differ.

SAMPLING — A DEFINITION

Sampling is a procedure familiar to all of us in many of its less precise forms. Tasting a spoonful of soup to see how well the whole pot is seasoned, examining a few apples to determine the quality of the entire bushel, or choosing one or two people to represent an entire category are instances of sampling. How often have you heard people make comments such as, "Just look at those two teenagers! What's the younger generation coming to?"

Some of these commonplace "samples" provide better bases for making generalizations than others. Intuitively, you would know that a spoonful of soup is likely to be an accurate reflection of the entire pot (assuming you have just stirred the soup), but that two teenagers do not accurately represent all teenagers. The soup sampling procedure is valid, because if we followed it again and again, each spoonful of soup would taste very much like the others. For the same reason, the haphazard selection of only two teenagers would be a poor sample, because if we repeated this procedure we would get widely different impressions from each pair of teenagers we picked. You cannot represent a group of people by looking at only one or two of its members because groups are seldom homogeneous. When dealing with human beings, you must sample a sufficient number of the group, using a procedure which ensures that each person has a known chance of selection.

SURVEY RESEARCH CENTER SAMPLING

One way to sample members of a group would be to write unique numbers for each member on identical slips of paper, then mix the slips in a giant container and draw again and again until a sufficient number of selections had been made. Obviously, it would take an inordinate amount of time and money to select dwellings in the United States in this manner. But since each dwelling can be associated with a specific region of the country, and since each region is divided into states, states are divided into counties, and counties, in turn, are divided into smaller units, we can save ourselves the expense and trouble of making a complete list. The Survey Research Center conducts a *multi-stage sampling of areas.* Sampling proceeds in stages, going from larger to smaller areas within the country. Roughly, the steps are as follows:

Step 1: Primary area selection. Coterminous United States is divided into what we call primary areas. These are generally counties, groups of counties, or metropolitan areas within which an interviewer can operate.

From these primary areas, we select at random (that is, by a probability method) 74 primary areas for the Center's national sample (Illustration 8-1).

The random selection process is not haphazard. Primary areas are selected by a mathematical procedure; each area has a known probability of selection, and there is no personal judgment involved. In the early stages of sampling we use a technique called *stratification,* which helps us select the proper proportion of primary areas from different types. When we stratify by region of the country, this means that a separate sample is drawn of Northeastern, Western, North Central, and Southern states, and each region has representation in proportion to its population.

Step 2: Sample location selection. Each one of the 74 selected primary areas is divided into smaller areas. Let us look at a hypothetical county, and see how it would be handled if it were selected as one of our 74 primary areas (Illustration 8-1).

Our hypothetical county consists of one large city, four medium-sized towns, and the remainder of the county. Three groups or strata would be formed on the basis of this information: large cities; smaller cities and towns; and remaining areas. One or more sample locations could then be selected within each stratum. The first stratum would include the large city, which becomes a sample location (since there is only one large city, there is no choice in this stratum); the

Illustration 8-1
SRC SAMPLING METHOD

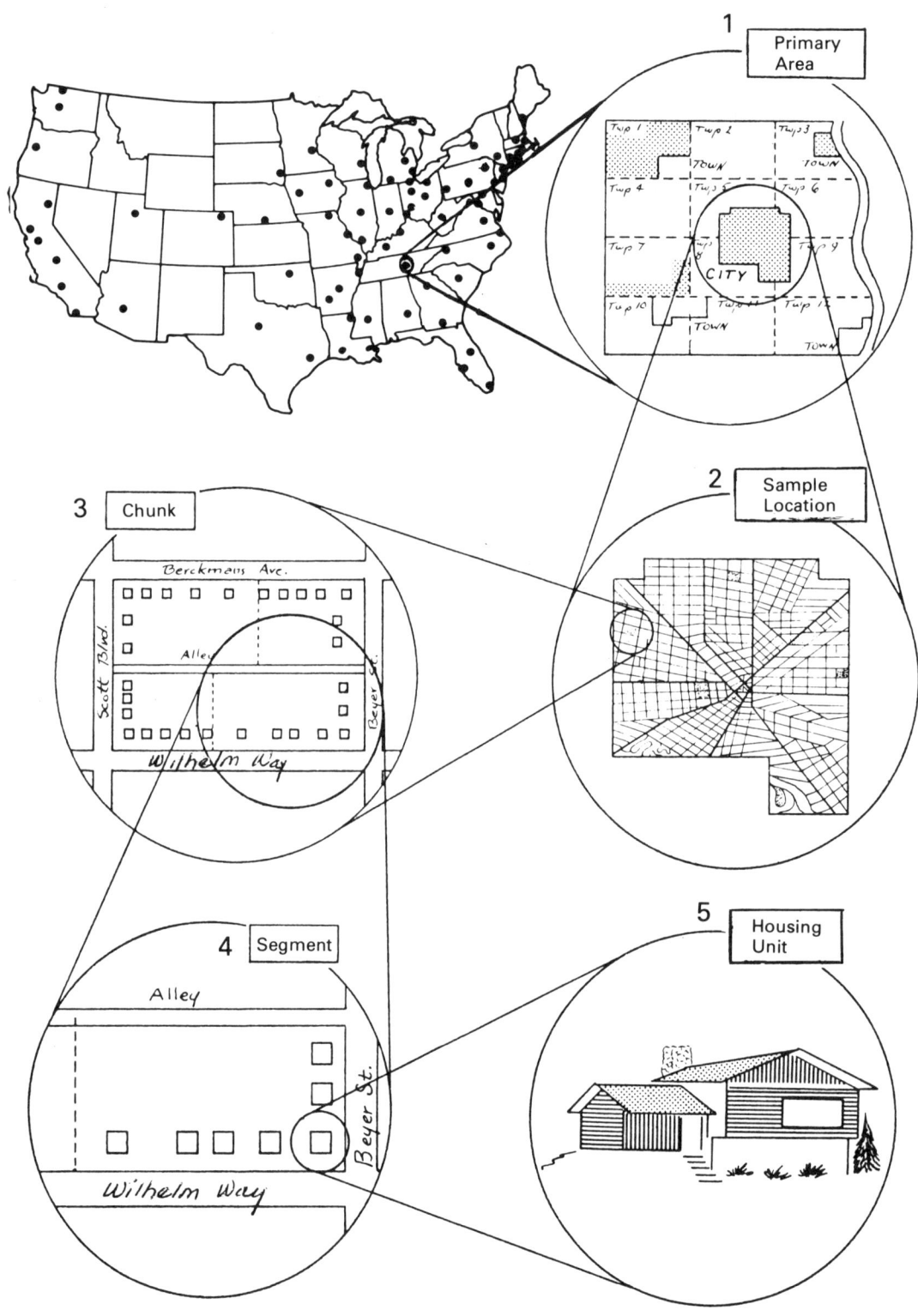

second stratum would consist of the four towns, and one or more of these would be selected. The third stratum would be the remainder of the county, all or part of which is designated as the third stratum sample location.

Step 3: Chunk selection. Each sample location, whether it is New York City or a rural township in Iowa, is divided into *chunks*. A chunk is a geographic area with identifiable (but not necessarily visible) boundaries; in a city or town it is usually a city block; in a rural area a chunk may be bounded by roads, natural features such as streams, or civil boundaries such as county lines. We try to make chunks that contain from 16 to 40 dwellings. In large cities, however, a chunk may have many more dwellings.

After all sample locations (cities, towns, and rural areas) have been divided into chunks, some of these chunks are selected — again by probability methods — for our sample.

Step 4: Segment selection. Before the Ann Arbor office can select compact areas for study, the interviewer must scout each sample chunk and either report addresses and estimates of the number of housing units (HU's) at each address, or shows the number and locations of HU's on a sketch of the chunk. (HU's are discussed fully in Chapter 9.) The interviewer must also suggest ways in which the chunk can be divided into smaller parts called *segments*. When this procedure is complete, the Ann Arbor office selects segments for each study.

Step 5: Housing unit selection. Within a segment, either all or part of the HU's, usually about four, are chosen for a specific study, although some studies require larger numbers of HU's from a segment. The interviewer is provided with specific instructions and has no personal choice in the selection of sample HU's.

THE INTERVIEWER AND THE SAMPLE

Occasionally, you may think that the segments which were chosen are not at all typical of the community. In most SRC surveys, the segments in a particular county or metropolitan area are not necessarily characteristic of that particular area because the purpose of the sample is not to represent one county, but rather to represent the entire United States, or major regions of it.

The following chapters describe ways in which to identify sample HU's and select respondents. In carrying out these procedures, *you must not substitute one HU for another if the original HU does not produce an interview.* If no one is home when you call, you must not step next door. The house on the muddy back road, the apartment at the top of a long flight of steps, the house with the growling dog outside must each have an opportunity to be included in the sample. People who live on back roads can be very different from people who live on well paved streets, and people who stay at home are not the same as those who tend to be away from home. If you make substitutions, such important groups as young men, people with small families, employed women, farmers who regularly trade in town, and so on, may not have proportionate representation in the sample.

SUMMARY

Sampling is the procedure we use to select certain members of a group to represent the entire group; the group of individuals selected is called a sample. Our procedure for selecting a sample is roughly as follows:

• The United States is divided into primary areas, usually by counties. Using a probability sampling method, 74 of these areas are selected as the Center's sample of primary areas.

• Then, particular *locations* (cities, towns, and rural areas) are selected within the primary areas.

• Chunks (geographical areas containing from 16 to 40 HU's) are selected within each sample location.

• The chunks are further divided into *segments* of from 4 to 16 HU's.

• A sample of HU's is drawn from segments.

Human judgment is not a reliable sampling technique, and you must not deviate from the specified selection of HU's. The accuracy of the sample depends to a large extent on the interviewers, and if surveys are to be effective, you must carry out correct sampling procedures carefully and conscientiously.

9 TYPES OF LIVING QUARTERS DEFINED

SRC national household samples are designed to represent the housing unit population in coterminous United States, exclusive of HU's on military reservations. For our purposes, living quarters in the United States fall into three general categories:
- Housing units (HU's)
- Excluded quarters
- Unclassified quarters, for which there is no obvious classification; details on these quarters are to be sent to the Ann Arbor office where a decision will be made.

HOUSING UNITS Housing units are defined by two general criteria: the fact that the living quarters are *used separately* by their occupants, and by certain *physical characteristics* of those quarters.

Operational Definition of a Housing Unit (HU) A housing unit is a room or group of rooms *occupied or vacant and intended for occupancy* as *separate living quarters*. In practice, living quarters are considered separate and therefore a housing unit when:

the occupants live and eat apart from any other group in the building,

AND THERE IS EITHER

direct access from the outside or through a common hall,

OR

complete kitchen facilities for the *exclusive use* of the occupants, regardless of whether or not they are used.

Occupants Live and Eat Apart Occupants are considered to be *living apart* from any other group in the building when they own or rent different living quarters. They are considered to be *eating apart* when they provide and prepare their own food *or* have complete freedom to choose when and where they eat, *and* they do *not* have to pay a fee for meals whether or not they are eaten.

Housing units may be occupied by a single family, or by two or more family units.

If a single building is occupied by persons or groups of people who live and eat apart from each other, the living quarters of each person or group are to be evaluated in accordance with the other HU criterion of direct access *or* complete kitchen facilities.

Direct Access Living quarters have direct access if there is EITHER:

an entrance directly from the outside of the building;

OR

an entrance directly from a common hall, lobby, or vestibule, used by the occupants of more than one unit or by the general public.

Access is *not* direct if, as the only means of access to the unit, the occupants *must* pass through another person's living quarters.

Complete Kitchen Facilities A unit has complete kitchen facilities when it has: an installed sink with piped water, *and* a range or cook stove, *and* a mechanical refrigerator. Portable cooking equipment does not qualify as a range or stove, nor is an ice box equivalent to a mechanical refrigerator. All kitchen facilities must be located in the building, but they need not be in the same room.

Kitchen facilities are for the exclusive use of the occupants when the living quarters are rented (or bought) with the understanding that the renter (or buyer) is not required to share kitchen facilities with other tenants.

INTERVIEWER'S MANUAL

Examples Most types of living quarters that meet the HU definition are easily identifiable. These are single family houses, row houses, town houses, duplexes, flats, garden-type apartments, apartments over commercial structures, high-rise apartments, and mobile homes.

EXCLUDED QUARTERS Certain types of *institutional* and *transient or seasonal facilities* which are never to be listed are called excluded quarters.

Institutional The institutional quarters which are to be excluded are those occupied or intended for occupancy by the persons for whom the facility is operated. Among these are: patient quarters in hospitals, rest homes, or nursing homes; quarters for the religious in cloistered convents or monasteries; student dormitories in schools or colleges, fraternities, or sororities; and inmates' quarters in mental or penal institutions.

Transient or Seasonal Transient or seasonal quarters are to be excluded if:

There are *five or more* units (whether beds, rooms, suites, cabins, trailers, tent or trailer sites, or boat moorings) operated *under a single management;*

AND

When the living quarters are EITHER:

—*transient;* that is, *more than 50 percent* of the units are normally occupied or intended for occupancy by persons who usually stay less than 30 days *or* who pay at a daily rate;

OR

—*seasonal;* that is, the facility is closed during at least one season of the year.

Transient or seasonal quarters to be excluded are: nonstaff accommodations in missions, flophouses, or Salvation Army shelters; accommodations for guests in *transient* hotels, motels, Y's, residential clubs, or resort establishments; vacation accommodations in campgrounds; transient trailer parks or marinas; and bunkhouses, cabins, trailers, and tents for migratory or seasonal workers.

Exceptions Within Excluded Quarters In facilities containing excluded institutional, transient, or seasonal quarters, check carefully for any living quarters which are occupied or intended for occupancy by resident owners or employees and their families. Staff quarters which meet the HU criteria are to be classified accordingly.

Institutionally operated student housing which meets the HU definition, such as married student apartment or trailers, is *not* to be excluded.

UNCLASSIFIED QUARTERS Unclassified quarters are living quarters that do not clearly meet the HU criteria, yet which are not clearly to be excluded. For these unconventional situations, a determination will be made by the Ann Arbor office.

10 SCOUTING THE CHUNK

Chunks are the smallest areas that we can identify from published materials, but they are too large for use on a single study. Therefore, we need to have interviewers scout these chunks and furnish information which will identify smaller areas, or segments, which can be selected for a few studies. These segments may vary in size, but they should have boundaries or limits which are clear enough and permanent enough to allow anyone to locate them now and in the future.

SEGMENT IDENTIFICATION

There are two procedures for dividing chunks into segments. Each one involves a different kind of scouting and each defines and identifies segments in a different way.

Area Procedure

During scouting, the interviewer estimates the number of HU's in various parts of the chunk, and notes on the sketch how the chunk might be divided into smaller pieces. This information is then sent to the Ann Arbor office and used to divide the chunk into identifiable geographic areas, or "area" segments.

Building Listing Procedure

During scouting, both residential and nonresidential buildings and all major land use are recorded on Building Listing Sheets (Form S220), along with a good estimate of the number of HU's in each building. These lists are sent to the Ann Arbor office where the listed entries are grouped into "building" segments.

MATERIALS

Before going into the field always make sure that you have a sufficient supply of the materials required to do the job. The mapping and listing required by scouting should be done at the sample site on the forms that are to be returned to Ann Arbor. Recopying takes time and increases the chance of error.

What You Will Receive from the Ann Arbor Office

- Transmittal Form (F151), "Summary of Sampling Materials" which lists by number the chunks enclosed for scouting. There is also a date shown when the work is to be completed and mailed to the Ann Arbor office.
- A Field Map on which the general location of each chunk is outlined in red (Illustration 10-7, page 52).
- A detailed drawing of the chunk, usually referred to as the chunk sketch (Illustration 10-9, page 54).
- Information Sheet for each chunk (yellow) (Illustrations 10-8 and 10-10, pages 53, 55, and 56).

What to Take with You

- The Field Map, chunk sketches, and Information Sheets.
- Lined pad, ruler.
- A supply of Building Listing Sheets — (Form S220) (Illustration 10-14, pages 61, 62, and 63).
- Pens or number 2 pencils. (The listings you send are reproduced in the Ann Arbor office for use here. The writing should be dark enough to make clear copies. A hard lead, number 3 pencil will not reproduce well.)

BECOME FAMILIAR WITH THE MAP

Study your map *before* you travel to the chunks and plan the most efficient way to get to the places where you will be working. The map you will be sent is the best map we have been able to locate. Please be on the alert for recently published maps for sample locations in your primary area. Send two copies to the Ann Arbor office and keep as many as you need for the primary area files.

INTERVIEWER'S MANUAL

The Difference Between Map and Chunk Sketches

For communication purposes between the staff in the field and the Ann Arbor office, it is important to know that when the word *map* is used, it refers to any *printed* map of an area, generally the map showing a chunk or group of chunks for a sample location. The word *sketch* describes a *hand-drawn* picture which is used for sampling purposes.

Map Symbols

Become familiar with the map symbols which are usually explained in a legend on the map sheet. The features they represent can serve as landmarks to help you locate a chunk or as reference points within the chunk. Often more or less permanent features such as schools, parks, etc., are shown as well as roads, civil boundaries, and geographical features.

Chunk Sketch Symbols

There are a few chunk sketch symbols, often used by the Ann Arbor office, with which you need to be acquainted. The symbol ⟋⟍, called a hitch, is used to show that the two parts of an area bisected by a road or stream have been joined. A dashed line ----- is used to show a property line or an imaginary line of sight. A wavy line ∿∿ is used by an interviewer to indicate that features shown on the chunk sketch, such as a road or railroad tracks, do not exist.

Map Scales and Chunk Sketch Scales

Maps usually have a scale. For example, one inch on the map may equal one mile on the ground. The scales will vary from map to map, but the principle is the same. Many chunk sketches also have a scale and you can use the scale to estimate the distance between any two points in a chunk.

KNOW THE HOUSING UNIT DEFINITION

You must know the definition of a housing unit; study Chapter 9 in this manual, "Types of Living Quarters Defined," so that you will know what to count as a housing unit when you are scouting.

CHECK THE BOUNDARIES

Check the chunk boundaries to make sure you have located the chunk correctly. Boundaries may be streets, roads, highways, railroad tracks, rivers, named streams, or other recognizable physical features. Boundaries may also be state or county lines, corporate limits, or other civil boundaries. On the sketch we have outlined the boundaries of the

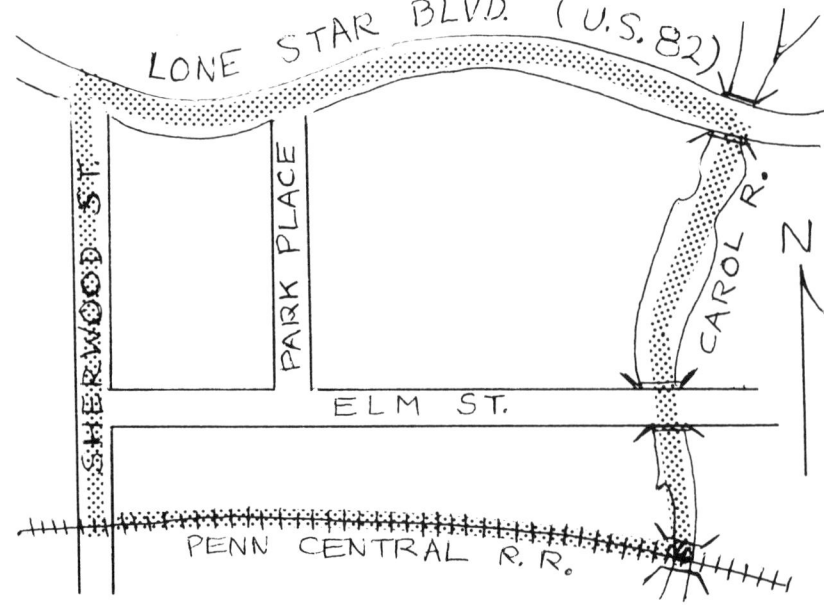

Illustration 10-1

CHUNK SKETCH SHOWING STREETS, RAILROAD, AND RIVER AS BOUNDARIES chunk in grey and included some of the physical features from the map. If there are no street names, highway numbers, etc., shown on the sketch, or if the local names differ from those which we have used, *please enter the correct names or numbers on the sketch.* Put a line through an incorrect street or highway name, but do not try to obliterate it. Where highways are identified by number, try to obtain the name of the street or road, since route numbers may change.

Civil Boundaries

Because we use some civil boundaries (city, county, and township lines) as they were at the time of the last decennial census, you may have difficulty locating them. Since cities and towns are constantly expanding, the posted boundaries at the time of scouting may not coincide with those we use. You should ask someone who knows (usually a city or county official) where the boundaries were located *as of the date specified on the chunk sketch.* Maps may be misleading when you are attempting to locate civil boundaries. For example, it may appear on the map that the boundary runs down the middle of a street, when in fact it runs along the back property line of the structures facing the street.

If the boundary appears to coincide with a road, stream, or other physical feature, inquire about its exact location; e.g., is it in the middle of the road, on the north edge of the right of way, the back property line of the lots on the north side, or where? (See Illustrations 10-2a and 10-2b.)

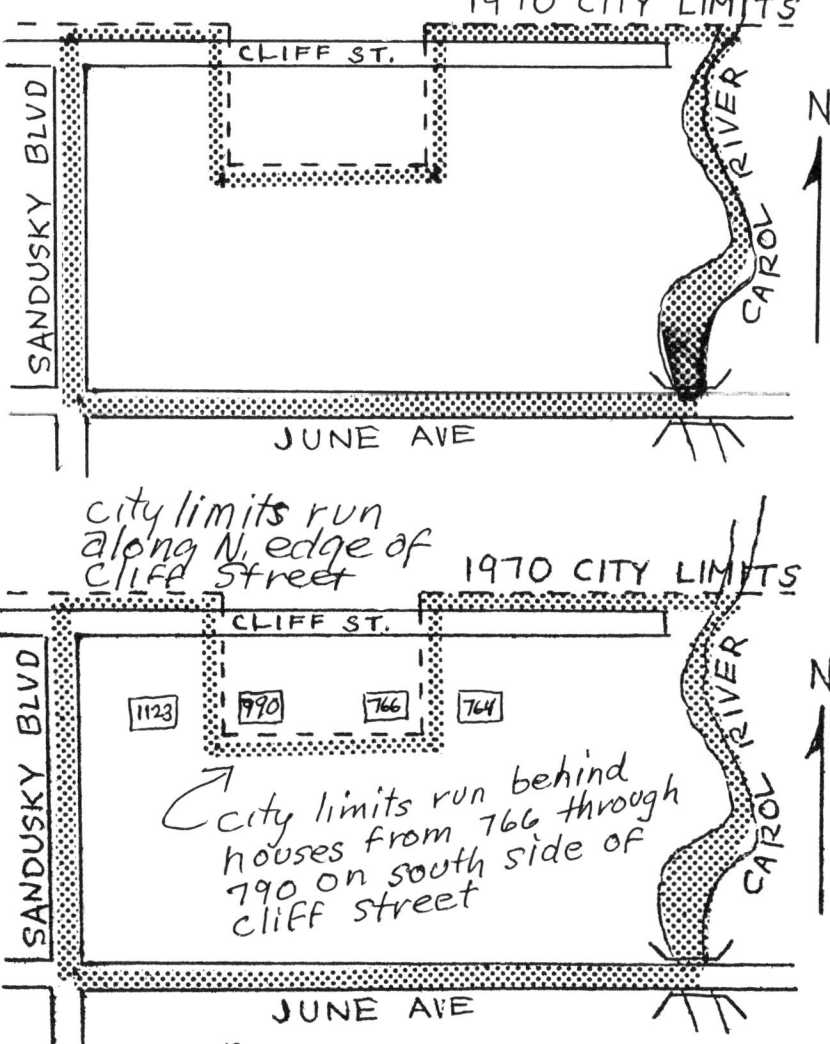

Illustration 10-2a

CHUNK SKETCH AS IT APPEARS WHEN SENT OUT FOR SCOUTING

Illustration 10-2b

CHUNK SKETCH AFTER INTERVIEWER HAS MADE INQUIRIES AND NOTED LOCATION OF 1970 CORPORATE LIMITS BY IDENTIFYING HOUSES ON EITHER SIDE

INTERVIEWER'S MANUAL

Boundaries That Do Not Exist

The preceding paragraphs imply that chunks always have identifiable boundaries; this is not always true, and a bit of skepticism about maps is not unhealthy. If we must make a choice between having the correct number of HU's and using firm, identifiable boundaries, *we prefer good boundaries,* and would increase the number of HU's from which to draw our sample if necessary. However, if we have used a civil boundary, that particular boundary *must be located and used,* no matter how difficult it is to find.

Sometimes maps show what the planning commission or a developer hoped would happen rather than what exists. If this is the case, use the following instructions:

- Locate the nearest potential boundaries.
- Indicate potential boundaries on a map or sketch, showing distances in miles, and distinguish them from other similar landmarks.
- Give estimates of the number of HU's in the area or show locations of HU's as now defined.
- If there is some doubt as to which of two features to choose as possible future boundaries, please report information about each.

INDICATE INTERNAL FEATURES

Look for the following types of features and show their location on the chunk sketch.

Internal Roads

You are to indicate all internal roads, streets, service roads, alleys, and those common walkways which connect parts of the chunk but do not run alongside streets. These provisions for the circulation of traffic within the segment form essential divisions when the building listing procedure is used and may be used as area segment boundaries.

Other Features That Divide the Chunk

Features which divide the chunk should also be indicated even though they are not used to get about the chunk. Examples of such features are limited access highways, rights of way for railroads and major power lines, rivers, streams, and other watercourses. These may be used in both scouting procedures for dividing the chunk and to serve as reference points in area segmenting.

Prominent Geographical Features

Other geographical features which limit the land use or movement within the chunk should be entered on the sketch or noted on the Information Sheet. Examples of such features are arroyos, deep ravines, canyons, escarpments, flood plains, and swamps.

Major New Construction

Use the Information Sheet attached to the chunk sketch to report major new construction such as apartment buildings, apartment complexes, housing developments, etc.

Street Names and House Numbers

Observe whether or not there are clear street names and an orderly arrangement of numbers for HU's in the chunk. These are points to consider when you are deciding whether to use the area or the building listing procedure to divide the chunk.

CHOOSE THE LISTING PROCEDURE TO USE

You must now decide whether to use the area procedure or the building listing procedure. If everything is clear, then the building listing procedure is the most efficient. The area segment procedure should be used if the chunk contains a fair number of HU's which do not have visible house numbers, or if HU's are located within the chunk in such a way that a list would not describe the chunk as clearly as would showing HU's or groups of HU's on the sketch with their approximate locations.

For most city and suburban blocks, the building listing procedure is the most efficient. For areas in which housing units must be accounted for with a written description because there are no street names or house numbers, the area procedure is best.

The decision is less clear for apartment complexes, townhouses, garden apartments, and housing developments. These arrangements of HU's may have street names and numbers or letters on the buildings and HU's, but it would probably be clearer to draw the buildings on the chunk sketch or to obtain a plat map from the management than it would be to try to list each building in an orderly fashion. In unusual chunks, both procedures might be called for — building listing in one part and area procedure in another. When there is any doubt, it is probably best to use the area procedure, since it is always appropriate even if it is not always the most efficient procedure.

SPECIAL CASES — APARTMENT BUILDINGS

Whichever procedure you choose, you must be familiar with the instructions for the cases listed below.

Report HU's on Each Floor of an Apartment Building

For each apartment building containing six or more HU's, record the address of the building, the number of floors, and the number of HU's on each floor. If you are listing buildings, record this information on the Building Listing Sheet with each floor listed on one line; otherwise, any sheet of lined paper can be used as a convenient reporting form. Attach this listing to the chunk sketch. If you find a five-story building and use a Building Listing Sheet, it might look like this:

(A)	(B) Address and/or description	(C) Approx. No. of HUs	(D)	(E)
	2041 N. Suffolk 1st Fl.	15		
	" lobby	10		
	" 2nd fl.	30		
	" 3rd fl.	30		
	" 4th fl.	26		

Illustration 10-3a

BUILDING LISTING SHOWING EACH FLOOR OF AN APARTMENT BUILDING LISTED SEPARATELY

We would like a fairly exact count of the number of HU's on each floor of any apartment building. You can usually obtain this information from a register just inside the entrance to the building, from mailboxes placed in a central location, or from the resident manager, doorman, or other attendant. As a last resort for estimating the number of floors and number of HU's in an apartment building, stand on the sidewalk outside and count the levels. Also supply your guess of the number of apartments per floor or of the total number of apartments in the structure, noting that it is an estimate. This will be better than no information at all.

Make a Sketch to Identify Floors in Large Apartment Buildings

To avoid confusion about the identification of floors in large apartment buildings, it is a good idea to draw a simple rectangle, indicate the street level(s) and label the floors using the same terminology as tenants use. This will help identify the sample selection and help the interviewer find the selected HU's when it is time to conduct interviews. Some buildings have a ground floor, a first floor, a mezzanine, and a second floor, while in other buildings the same arrangement would designate the floors as one through four.

INTERVIEWER'S MANUAL

A labeled sketch is particularly helpful when there are several floors of apartments over stores. The statement "2nd floor above stores" is ambiguous.

Estimate HU's Within Small Multi-Unit Apartment Buildings

In some chunks there may be several small multi-unit structures containing from two to five HU's. Neighborhoods which appear to contain all single family HU's can be deceptive. The number of mailboxes, electric meters, doorbells, or garbage cans may suggest the presence of more than one HU in a structure and help you estimate the number of HU's. If necessary ask someone how many apartments are in the structure.

SPECIAL CASES — EXCLUDED QUARTERS

You will need to make detailed inquiries to determine whether some types of places are to be included or excluded from your estimate. Identify and locate the facility, but count only owner, manager, and staff living quarters in excluded facilities. Refer to the section on "EXCLUDED QUARTERS" in Chapter 9 of this manual.

Note Whether Trailer Courts, Resorts, Motels, and Hotels Are for Permanent, Transient, or Seasonal Guests

For each trailer court, resort, motel, and hotel, we need to know the number of housing units or trailer spaces (cabins, rooms, suites, or other accommodations) for *permanent* residents and the number for *transients*. Include the owner's or manager's living quarters (trailer, apartment, or house) in the count of units for permanent residents. You will also need to know whether or not the facility operates throughout the year or if it is only open for part of the year.

Illustration 10-3b

INTERVIEWER'S SKETCH IDENTIFYING THE ARRANGEMENT OF FLOORS WITHIN AN APARTMENT

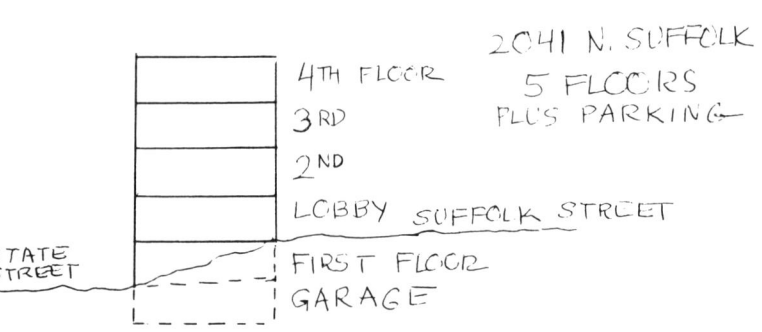

Trailer Courts for Residents

Please provide a rough sketch or plat map showing the rows of trailer spaces and the number of trailer spaces per row (Illustration 10-12, page 58).

Trailer Courts for Transients

See the discussion of transient or seasonal HU's on page 40. Describe the situation in Item E on the Information Sheet for the chunk.

Scouting the Chunk

Apartment (Residential) Hotels

If 50 percent or more of the accommodations (rooms, suites) in a hotel are occupied or intended for occupancy by nontransient residents, we consider the building an *apartment hotel,* and it is treated like any other apartment building — tell us how many floors there are and how many HU's per floor.

Hotels for Transients

If 50 percent or more of the accommodations (rooms, suites) in a hotel are occupied or intended for occupancy by *transient* guests, the structure is referred to as a "hotel," and should be excluded from our household samples. Remember, however, that the owner's, manager's, or other staff members' quarters in the hotel are included. See discussion of transient or seasonal HU's on page 40.

Distinguish Between Apartments and Homes for the Elderly (Institutions)

In apartments, occupants have complete freedom to choose when and where they eat. If a fee is charged for meals, the unit should be considered an institution. Refer to the section on "HOUSING UNITS" in Chapter 9 of this manual.

AREA PROCEDURE

When you are using the area procedure, your main job is to divide the chunk into segments of about 4 to 12 housing units. In order to do this with reasonable accuracy and efficiency you will need to:

- Update the chunk sketch.
- Make approximate counts of housing units.
- Select clear segment boundaries.
- Draw segment boundaries on the chunk sketch, label them clearly, and show other information which will help you and other interviewers locate HU's in the segments.
- Show the total number of HU's and racial composition on the chunk sketch.
- Complete the Information Sheet for each chunk.

Update the Chunk Sketch

The published maps from which the chunk sketch is drawn are often outdated and inaccurate. Since the chunk sketch will be the basic document for future sampling, it must locate and identify boundaries and internal roads. See "CHECK THE BOUNDARIES" (pages 42 and 43).

Make Approximate Counts of HU's

In scouting it is not necessary for the HU counts to be absolutely perfect. If an occasional HU is missed, it can be added in the segment listing and interviewing stages. However, consistent underreporting or overreporting of the number of HU's in the chunks increases variation in the sample size. This can be troublesome to interviewers because study assignments will be larger or smaller than anticipated. A good method of accounting for HU's as you scout is to locate each HU on the sketch by drawing a small square. If a building contains more than one HU, indicate the approximate number by writing it over the square. Since HU's are seldom distributed evenly around any chunk, the sketch may become cluttered and unclear if you attempt to draw a square for each HU in the most densely populated portions. Do not distort the map scale to make room for squares. Instead, omit all but the squares which anchor segment boundaries, or use a separate piece of paper to show an enlargement of the congested part of the segment.

INTERVIEWER'S MANUAL

Select Clear Segment Boundaries

It is more important to establish boundaries which are permanent, unambiguous, and easy to locate than it is to create segments of equal size. Because of this, we allow a range of from 4 to 12 HU's for each segment, but this may be different for some scouting assignments. Use permanent features, imaginary lines, and back property lines for boundaries.

Permanent Features

The best segment boundaries are easily recognizable and relatively permanent features such as roads, railroads, streets, alleys, named creeks, rivers, irrigation ditches, and major power transmission lines. Fence lines and tree lines may be used, but these are less apt to be permanent. See the discussion of chunk boundaries on pages 42, 43, and 44 in this chapter.

Imaginary Lines

Imaginary lines of sight between identifiable points on the gound may be used as segment boundaries in the *absence* of natural boundaries. Extensions of streets and roads are to be projected from the center line of the existing street. Lines of sight along the side of clearly identified HU's are also acceptable. If you cannot sight from the beginning point of an imaginary boundary line to the point at which it intersects another boundary, check the probable point of intersection by referring to the sketch or sample location maps, or by taking odometer readings along the sides of the segment. If you can locate the approximate intersection and if you feel certain that another interviewer could also locate this intersection, then use the imaginary line as a segment boundary (or part of one). The point at which an imaginary boundary intersects a street or road must always be identified clearly.

Back Property Lines

Another kind of imaginary line which may be used as a segment boundary is a back property line. These lines, even if they are not marked by fences, are usually clear in the layout of the neighborhood. HU's are seldom built close enough to back property lines to cause problems at the time of listing or updating.

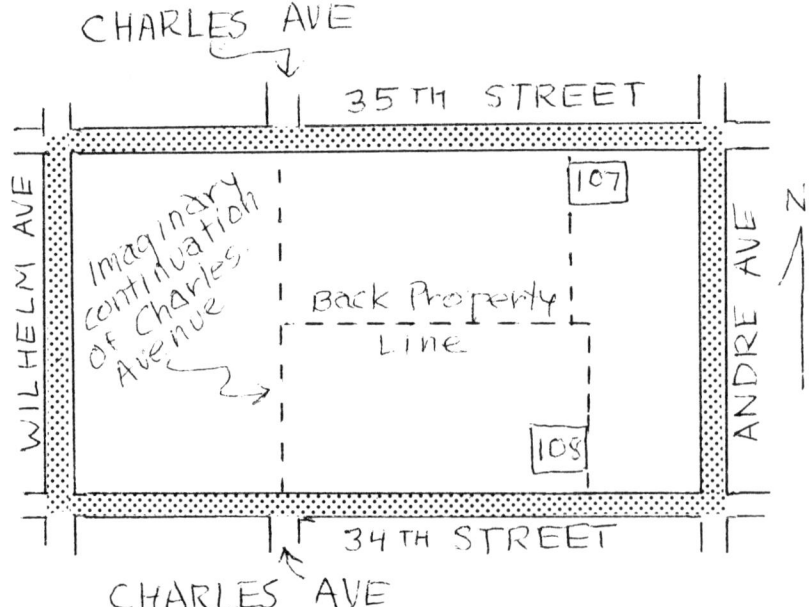

Illustration 10-4

CHUNK SKETCH SHOWING USE OF COMMON BACK PROPERTY LINE, EXTENSION OF A STREET, AND IMAGINARY LINES BESIDE HOUSES AS SEGMENT BOUNDARIES

Scouting the Chunk

If a Chunk Cannot be Divided

If all of our suggestions fail and you cannot find a way to divide the chunk or some part of it into segments, list each dwelling on any lined paper, number the lines, and indicate the location of each HU on the chunk sketch with a square. On the sketch, write the line number of the HU which corresponds to the line number on the listing sheet.

Draw Segment Boundaries on the Chunk Sketch

The boundaries you select must be identified clearly by locating them on the sketch and labeling them accurately. Show any other helpful information, such as the mileage between boundaries, or landmarks which help locate the segment. If you are using imaginary boundary lines, indicate these with dashed lines on the sketch.

Show Total Number of HU's and Racial Composition of Segments

Assign a racial compositon for each segment by observation. Do not make inquiries. Record the code within the segment boundaries and next to the HU estimate on the chunk sketch. The notation ⑫ W-B would indicate that there are an estimated 12 HU's in the segment and that the racial composition is mixed.

Category	Code
Entirely white	W
Entirely black	B
Mixed	W-B
Not ascertained	NA

In Illustration 10-5, the interviewer divided the area into two segments by using an imaginary line along the south side of the school and to the north of an HU on County Line Road. To pin down the intersection on the eastern boundary, the interviewer not only described the anchor HU, but also used odometer readings from the intersection of Green Road and County Line Road. After locating residential buildings by drawing squares on the chunk sketch and adding landmarks such as the school, the interviewer noted the number of HU's and the racial composition within each segment. In the illustration, the segment on the north has an estimated four HU's (the number circled), and the racial composition is white. Note the semi-circular driveway off Wade Road and the two small multi-unit buildings. Each building contains three apartments; the interviewer indicated this by writing "3" over the square on the sketch.

Illustration 10-5

CHUNK SKETCH SHOWING USE OF ODOMETER READINGS TO PINPOINT BOUNDARIES AND METHOD OF INDICATING HU COUNTS AND RACIAL COMPOSITION WITHIN SEGMENTS

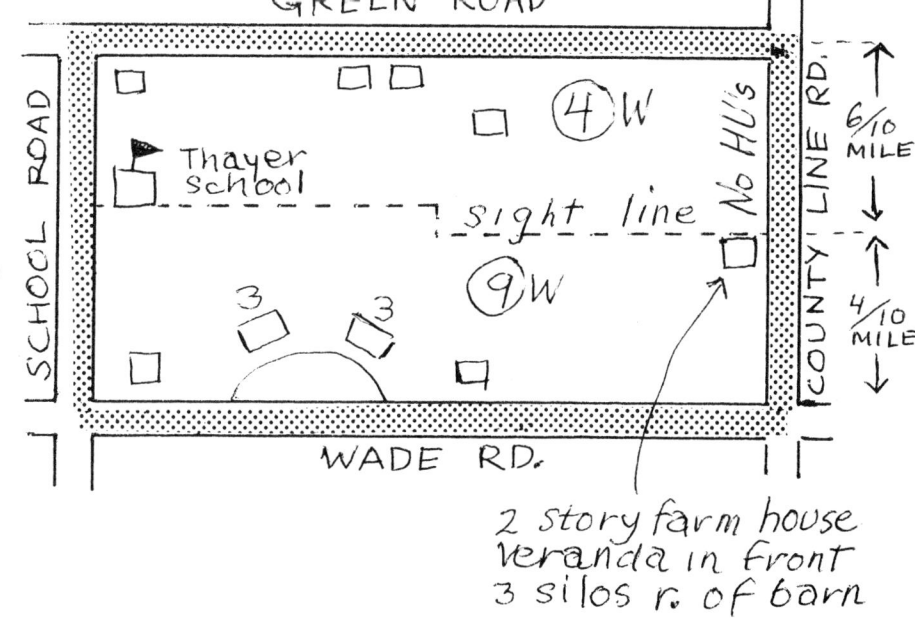

INTERVIEWER'S MANUAL

Complete the Information Sheet

When you have finished scouting the chunk, complete the Information Sheet (Illustrations 10-8 and 10-10). Be sure to put your interviewer's label in the space provided and record the date the work is completed so that we will know with whom to communicate if there are any questions or if we need further information.

Item A: Record the total number of HU's you estimate are in the chunk. If your estimate falls outside of the range we have allowed, explain the discrepancy on the back of the sheet under "COMMENTS."

Item B: Indicate which sampling procedure you decided to use.

Item C: Report new construction by type and stage of development.

Item D: Report any major demolition.

Item E: Report on vacation or seasonal use of HU's in the chunk.

Item F: In many cases you are not going to be able to determine the ethnic composition by observation, but if you are familiar with the neighborhood, give your impression of the racial and ethnic composition by segment.

Item G: These are broad income levels; if there is variation within the chunk, give the income level by segment.

Return Materials to Ann Arbor

When you have completed the scouting, return to the Ann Arbor office:

- The Field Map.
- The chunk sketch.
- The completed Information Sheet.
- Any additional notes, sketches, enlargements, etc. that you feel would be useful to describe the chunk.

Illustrations

Illustrations 10-6 through 10-12 are examples showing one chunk, in a semirural area, which was sent out to the field for scouting and which the interviewer divided using the area procedure.

- *Transmittal Form F151 (10-6)*. The project number 459160 is used only for scouting. Notice that Field Maps have been sent out for Jefferson City and also for a nonurban area designated as "remainder." Plan your work so that as many chunks as possible are scouted on each trip and so that the work is completed and mailed on or before the date requested. Supervisors receive a copy of the transmittal form; if there are reasons why you cannot mail the work by the deadline, notify the supervisor at once.

- *Field Map (10-7)*. The chunks to be scouted have been outlined on the Field Map.

- *Information Sheet (10-8)*. This sheet is for Chunk 8005 as it looked when it was sent out to the interviewer for scouting.

- *Chunk Sketch (10-9)*. Shows the sketch for Chunk 8005 as it looked when it was sent out to the interviewer for scouting.

- *Completed Information Sheet (10-10)*. The interviewer completed the Information Sheet after scouting the chunk.

- *Completed Chunk Sketch (10-11)*. The grey lines are the interviewer's notations for suggested segment boundaries. Because of the marshy interior of the chunk and the distances involved, an imaginary line or line of sight was not a practical boundary for some segments. The interviewer located all HU's on the chunk sketch and returned the work to Ann Arbor. In a situation such as this one, we can make the final decision about

Illustration 10-6
TRANSMITTAL FORM

FORM F151 - Transmittal (3-75)

Survey Research Center
University of Michigan

Project No. 459160

PSU Jefferson, Indiana

Date Dec. 10, 1974

SUMMARY OF SAMPLING MATERIALS
(FOR SCOUTING)

Place	Chunks (includes all types)	Map	Other (specify)	Materials Enclosed	Materials To Follow
1	2	3	4	5	6
Jefferson City	6001, 6002, 6003, 6004, 6005, 6006, 6007, 6008	X		X	
Remainder	8001, 8002, 8003, 8004, 8005, 8006, 8007, 8008, 8009, 8010, 8011, 8012	X		X	

PLEASE COMPLETE THE ABOVE ASSIGNMENT AND RETURN TO ANN ARBOR BY JANUARY 6. THANK YOU

INTERVIEWER'S MANUAL

Illustration 10-7
PORTION OF FIELD MAP LOCATING CHUNK 8005

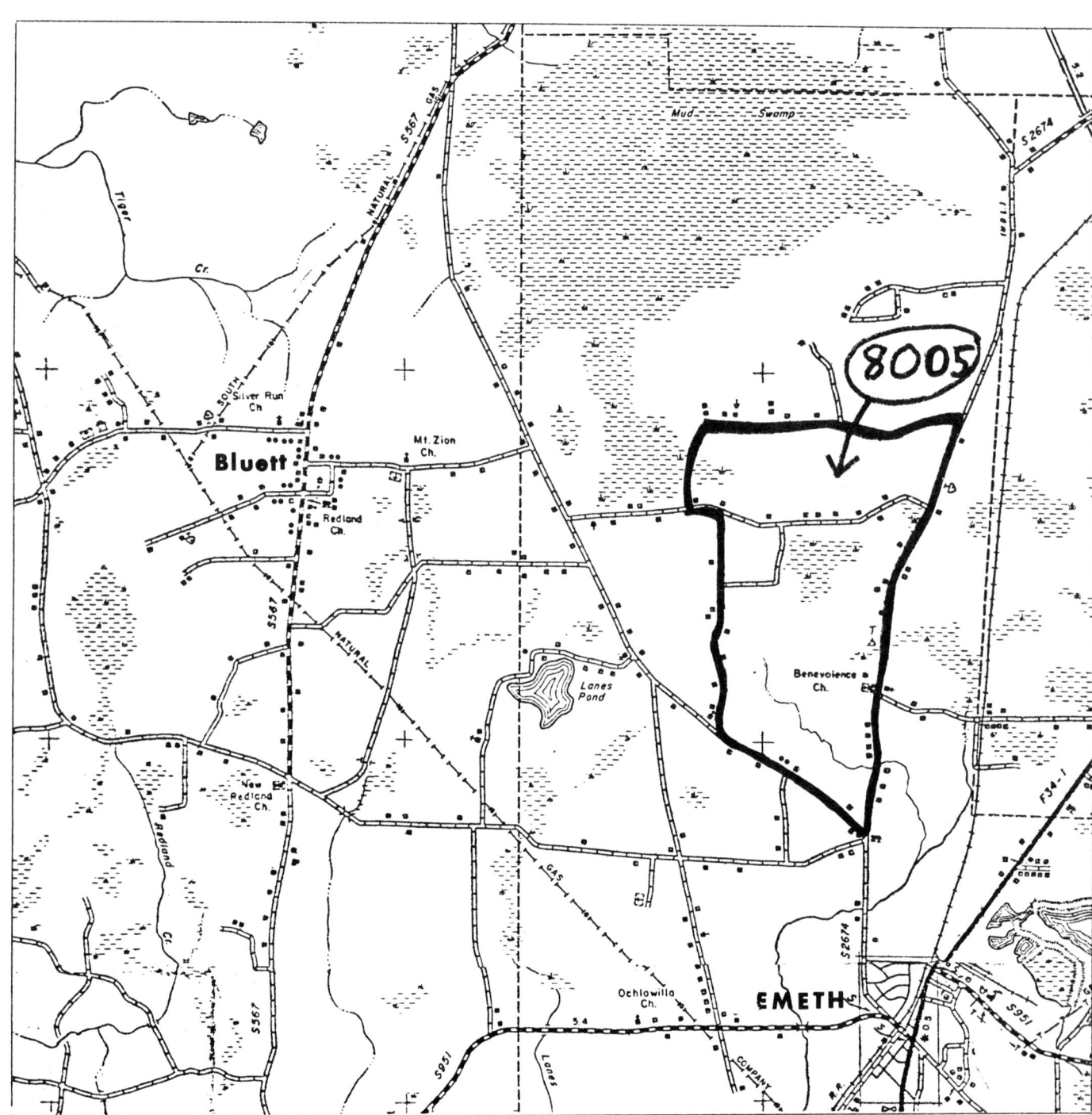

INFORMATION SHEET Illustration 10-8 Survey Research Center
The University of Michigan
FRONT SIDE OF INFORMATION SHEET AS RECEIVED (2/6/75)

Primary Area **Jefferson, Ind**

Sample Location **Remainder**

Chunk Number **8005**

Interviewer Label

Date: _____

A. NUMBER OF HU's IN CHUNK

Our estimate **32**; number you find _____.

If you find more than **64** or fewer than **16** please give probable

explanation for discrepancy. (Use back of sheet.)

B. SUGGESTED SAMPLING PROCEDURE

We suggest: ☒ Area Segment   ☐ Building Listing

Procedure used: (Specify)   ☐ Area Segment   ☐ Building Listing

C. NEW CONSTRUCTION INFORMATION

☐ 1. No evidence of new construction either underway or planned.

☐ 2. Some new construction underway or planned.
Describe: a) type and b) stage of development below.

    a. TYPE (Check one or more, as appropriate)

        ☐ (1) Single-family housing, major development

        ☐ (2) Low-rise (Garden, Townhouse, Terrace) apartment development. Approximate number of HUs _____

        ☐ (3) High-rise apartments. Approximate number of HU's _____

        ☐ (4) Minor construction--scattered housing units

    b. STAGE OF DEVELOPMENT (Check one or more, as appropriate)

        ☐ (1) Building started

        ☐ (2) Site preparation only, e.g., grading, clearing land, streets, etc.

        ☐ (3) Announced--on radio, TV, newspaper, billboards, or signs in area

        ☐ (4) Rumored but no formal announcement

Illustration 10-9
CHUNK SKETCH AS RECEIVED

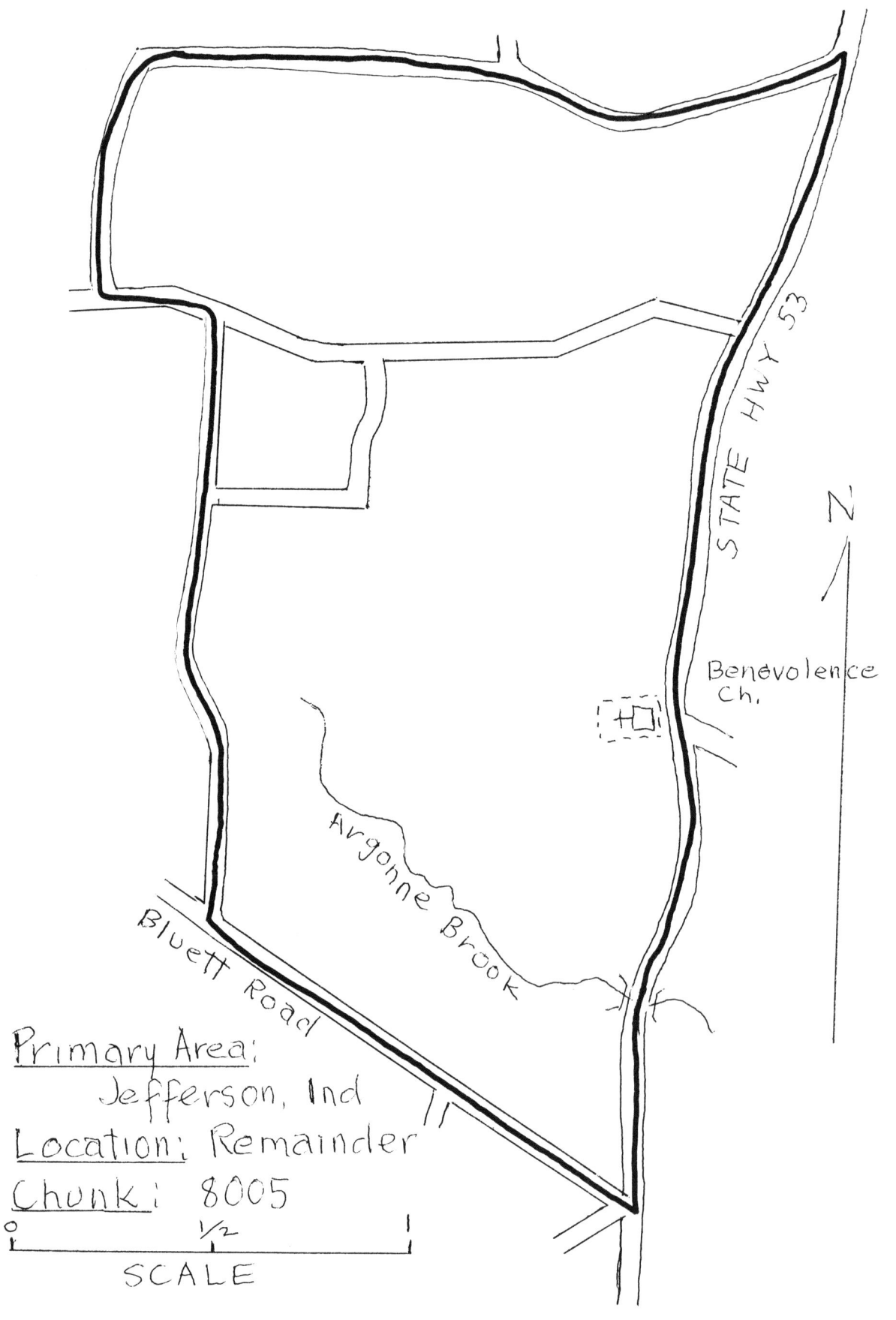

INFORMATION SHEET   Illustration 10-10a   Survey Research Center
                          INFORMATION SHEET COMPLETED (FRONT)   The University of Michigan
                                                                          (2/6/75)

Primary Area **Jefferson, Ind**
                                        562-30-7464   POTTER, BEATRICE
Sample Location **Remainder**   129 WISTFUL VISTA
                                                       JEFFERSON CITY, IND.
Chunk Number **8005**   47130

                                        Date: _____

A. NUMBER OF HU's IN CHUNK

   Our estimate **32**; number you find **50**.

   If you find more than **64** or fewer than **16** please give probable

   explanation for discrepancy. (Use back of sheet.)

B. SUGGESTED SAMPLING PROCEDURE

   We suggest: ☒ Area Segment   ☐ Building Listing

   Procedure used: (Specify) ☒ Area Segment   ☐ Building Listing

C. NEW CONSTRUCTION INFORMATION

   ☐ 1. No evidence of new construction either underway or planned.

   ☒ 2. Some new construction underway or planned.
        Describe: a) type and b) stage of development below.

      a. TYPE (Check one or more, as appropriate)

         ☐ (1) Single-family housing, major development

         ☐ (2) Low-rise (Garden, Townhouse, Terrace) apartment
               development. Approximate number of HUs _____

         ☐ (3) High-rise apartments. Approximate number of HU's _____

         ☒ (4) Minor construction--scattered housing units

      b. STAGE OF DEVELOPMENT (Check one or more, as appropriate)

         ☒ (1) Building started **Foundations poured**

         ☐ (2) Site preparation only, e.g., grading, clearing land,
               streets, etc.

         ☐ (3) Announced--on radio, TV, newspaper, billboards, or
               signs in area

         ☐ (4) Rumored but no formal announcement

Illustration 10-10b
INFORMATION SHEET COMPLETED (BACK)

D. **MAJOR DEMOLITIONS**

☒ 1. No evidence of major demolition

☐ 2. Some demolition underway or planned. (Describe by segment or listing sheet line as appropriate.)

E. **VACATION OR OTHER SEASONAL UNITS**

☐ 1. More than 50% of the HU's are seasonal units for (check a, b <u>or</u> c):

    ☐ a. Vacation use   ☐ b. Migrant workers   ☐ c. Some vacation some migrant

☐ 2. There are some seasonal units but they are less than 50% of all HU's

☒ 3. There are few or no seasonal units

F. **ETHNIC COMPOSITION OF CHUNK** (Check as many as apply)

☒ 1. White-W   ☒ 2. Black-B   ☐ 3. Spanish speaking-Sp

☐ 4. Asian-A: Japanese, Chinese, Asian Indian, Phillipino, etc.

☐ 5. Other race or language. Specify: _____

If more than one square is checked:

☐ 1. Groups are mixed evenly around the chunk;

☒ 2. Each group is clustered in particular parts of the chunk; indicate race or language by segment or by listing sheet line.

Blacks along Nixon Rd.

G. **ECONOMIC RATING** (Check the box that best describes the income level of households

☒ 1. LOW (Under $7,000)   ☐ 2. MEDIUM ($7,000-$19,999)   ☐ 3. HIGH ($20,000 OR OVER)   ☐ 4. Can't tell

COMMENTS: *Center of Chunk very swampy with no good boundaries*

Illustration 10-11
CHUNK SKETCH COMPLETED

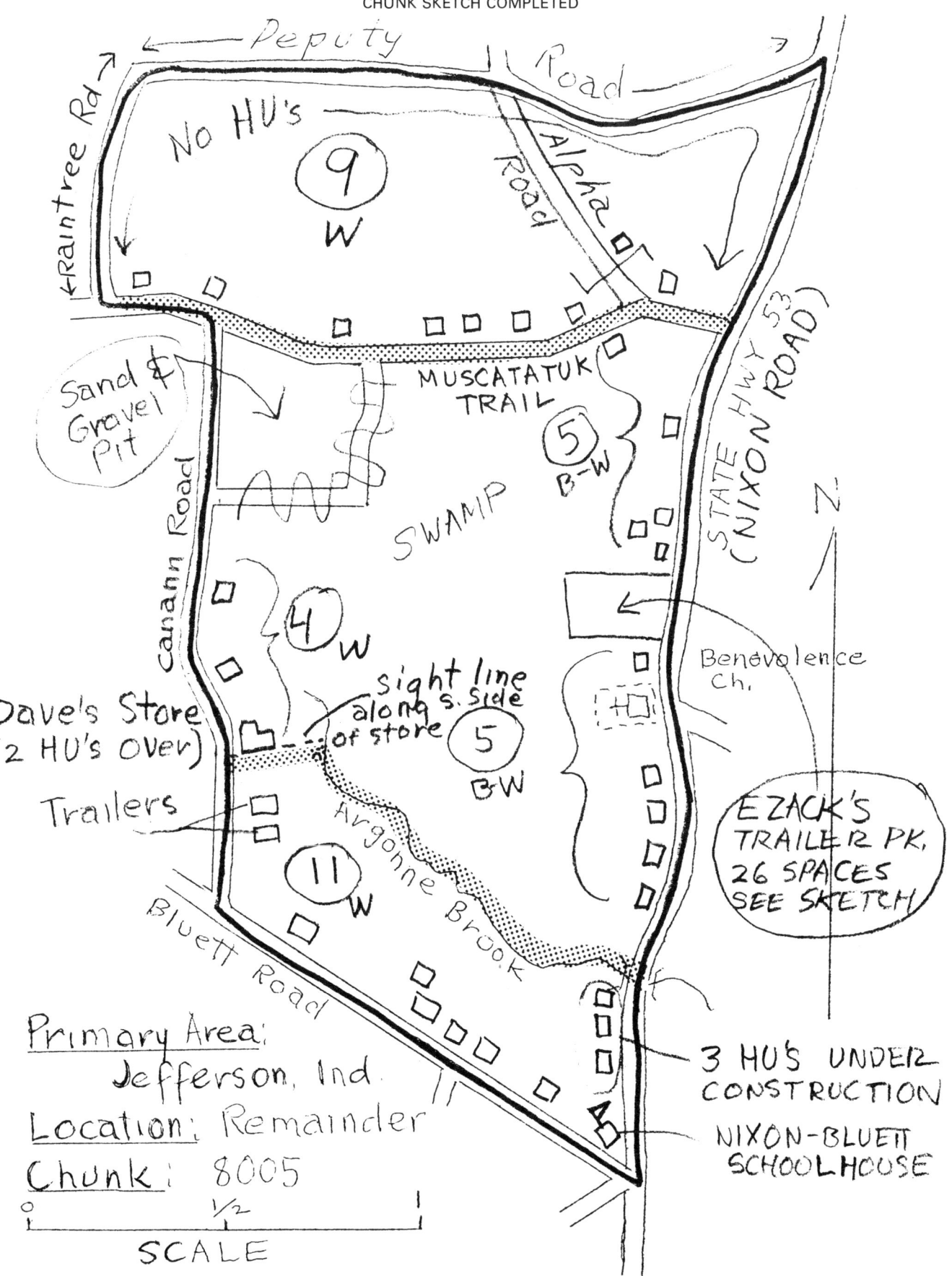

Illustration 10-12
INTERVIEWER'S SKETCH OF TRAILER PARK

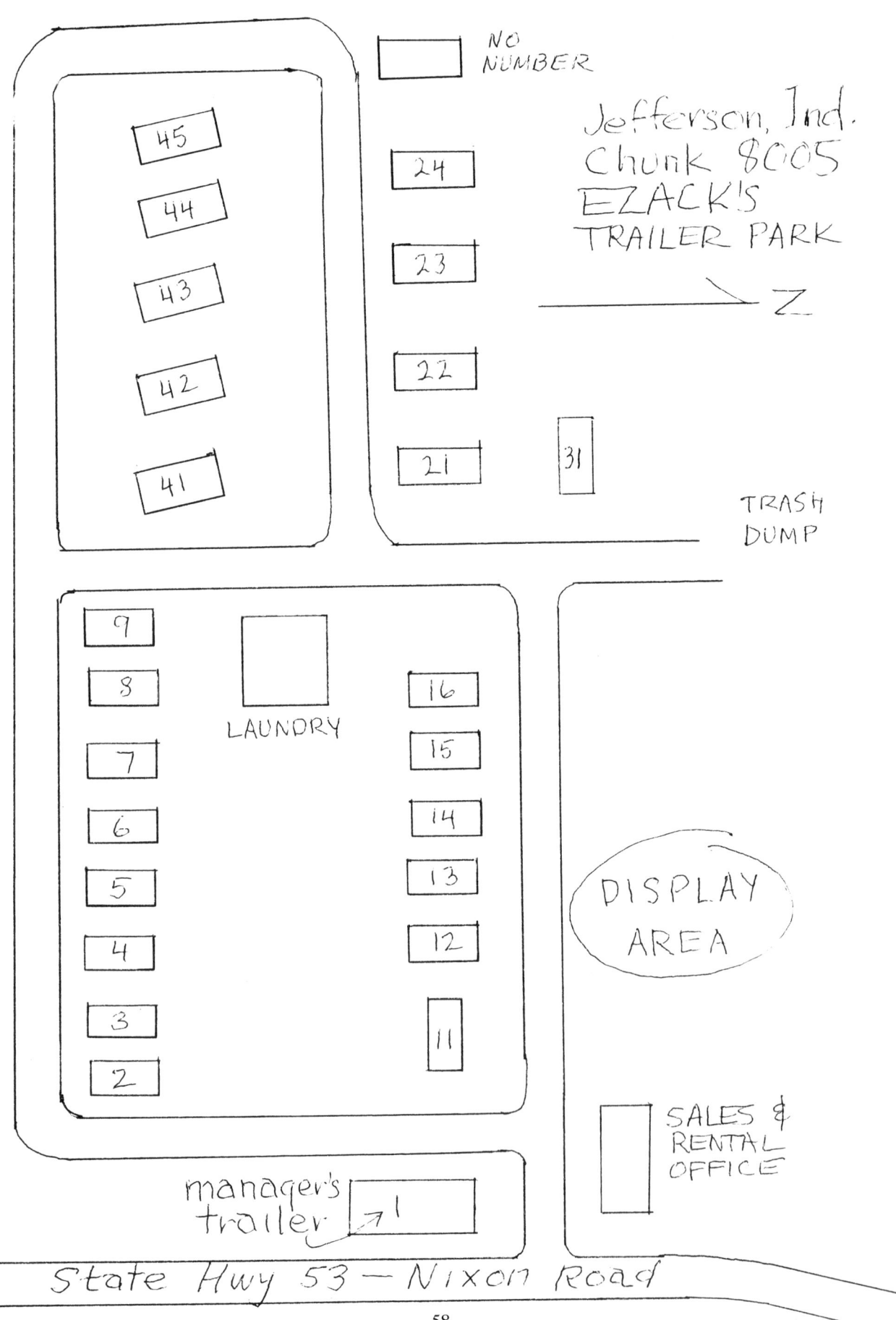

Scouting the Chunk

segment boundaries based on complete information from the interviewer. It is useful to know that the interviewer checked along the northern boundary and found no HU's. A line of sight (indicated by a grey line) from Bluett Road along the south side of Dave's store to Argonne Brook completed one of the segment boundaries.

- *Sketch (Plat Map) of Trailer Park (10-12).* The interviewer sketched a plat map of the trailer park showing the location of the trailer spaces and the "house" or "pad" numbers which the management of the park had assigned to the spaces. This sketch was attached to the chunk sketch and Information Sheet when they were returned to Ann Arbor.

BUILDING LISTING PROCEDURE

When you are using the building listing procedure, your job is to:

- Identify divisions within the chunk.
- Mark starting point on the sketch and indicate path.
- Identify on Building Listing Sheets *all* of the buildings in the chunk, both residential and nonresidential, *and* all major land use.
- Record the approximate number of HU's in each building.
- Complete the Information Sheet for this chunk.
- Return all required materials to Ann Arbor on or before the date given on the Transmittal Form.

Identify Divisions Within the Chunk

When you find that a chunk is divided by a street or alley, LIST EACH PART OF THE CHUNK SEPARATELY. (See page 44 "Internal Roads" and "Other Features That Divide the Chunk.") Identify each separate part (or subpiece) with a Roman numeral, USE SEPARATE BUILDING LISTING SHEETS FOR EACH PART, and at the top of each listing sheet, make a rough sketch of the part being listed. (See Illustration 10-14, pages 61, 62, and 63.)

If you find you need two or more S220 sheets to list a chunk or part of a chunk, be sure all the continuation sheets include the following information: primary area name, sample location name, chunk number, and the number of the S220 sheet in the space at the bottom: "Sheet ___ of ___."

Mark Starting Point on the Sketch and Indicate Path

Find a suitable starting place in each division of the chunk, such as the intersection of two boundaries; identify this point with an "X" on the sketch, and begin listing in a *clockwise* direction. If it is possible, avoid selecting a structure with addresses on two streets as a starting point. If you *must* use such a structure, include both addresses at the beginning of the listing sheet and bracket them. Proceed around the chunk, listing as you go and traveling into and out of any courts or dead end streets, as shown in Illustration 10-13. With small arrows on the sketch, show the path of your listing.

List all of the Buildings in the Chunk

List each building *or separate address* on a separate line of the Building Listing Sheet, either by address or, if there is no address, by a description. *Do not* guess at numbers. If the number is not visible, give a *brief* description of the building even though it is located between clearly numbered buildings. For example, the numbers on Floyd St. (Illustration 10-14), are 101, 103, 105, no number (describe), 109, 111. LIST BUILDINGS WHETHER OR NOT THEY CONTAIN HOUSING UNITS. List shops, stores, factories, service stations, etc., as well as residential structures. Use a black pen or soft (number 2) pencil when listing.

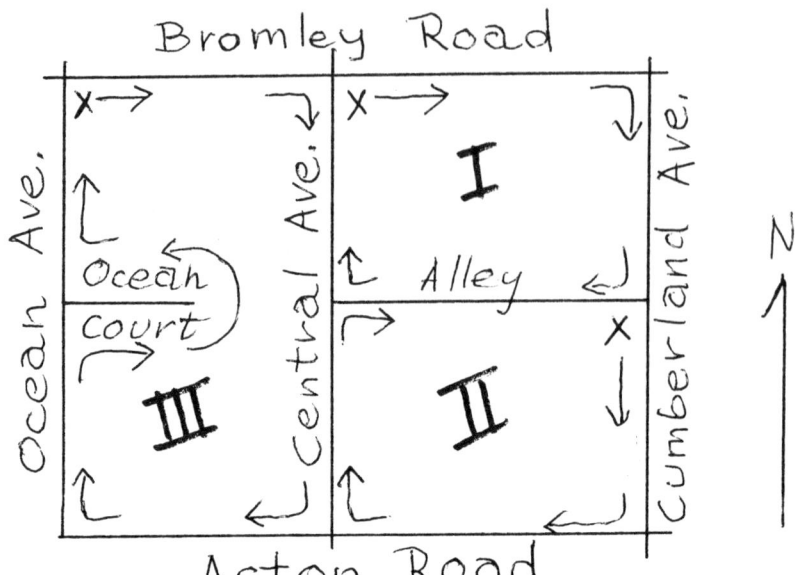

Illustration 10-13

CHUNK SKETCH FOR BUILDING LISTING SHOWING NUMBERED PARTS AND LINE OF TRAVEL

Identify Commercial Firms

If a building contains a commercial firm, include the name or a brief description along with the address; e.g., Nate's Boat Shop, Acme Motel, grocery store, dress shop, Willow Trailer Court, etc.

Structures not to List

Do *not* list service buildings which are associated with an adjoining listed building if they are not intended for human habitation. This includes detached garages which do not contain HU's, farm buildings adjacent to a farmhouse, storage sheds, etc., if you have listed the building with which they are associated.

Record the Approximate Number of HU's in Each Building

When you are listing the buildings, note and write in column C of the Building Listing Sheet your best estimate of the number of HU's each building contains. Refer to Chapter 9 for the definition of an HU and hints on locating obscure HU's.

List Large Buildings by Floor

When you find a building that seems to contain more than six HU's, list each floor on a separate listing line, and report the number of HU's per floor in column C. (See Illustration 10-3a on page 45.)

Bracket Listings in the Same Building

Whenever the situation warrants it, indicate with a bracket to the right of the listings that several listings are in the same building (Illustration 10-14).

Duplexes which have separate addresses are to be listed on two lines and joined by brackets. If a building on a corner has addresses on two streets, bracket all the addresses in that building.

Other Information to Enter on Building Listing Sheet

Specify on the Building Listing Sheet those streets which have no buildings. Also note such phenomena as narrow-ended blocks where there are no buildings because there is no room. Try to indicate where there are vacant lots or areas where building might occur in the future, as well as any kind of land use which explains why there are no buildings in an area. Note for example such land uses as:

- Vacant lots, farmland, undeveloped land.
- Parking lots — you need not make note of parking lots adjoining businesses or associated with shopping centers, churches, or

Illustration 10-14a
COMPLETED BUILDING LISTING FOR A THREE PART CHUNK

BUILDING LISTING SHEET

Primary Area **Henley, Nev.**
Location **Carsonville**
Chunk **6003**
Estimated HUS **38**
Census Tract _____
Census Block _____

Survey Research Center
The University of Michigan
Date **Sept. 20, 1973**
Lister **Doris Darrah**

(A)	(B) Address and/or Description (specify street number; street, avenue, or boulevard, etc.; and whether north or south, etc.)	(C) Approx. No. of HUS	(D)	(E)
I	232 Church St Golden Standard Station	0		
	234 L & L Grocery	0		
	236	1		
	238	1		
	240 storefront converted to apartment } commercial building with upstairs apts enter off Floyd St.	1		
	242 Nugget Cleaners	0		
	101 Floyd St.	3		
	103	1		
	105	1		
	Brown brick, 1 story, slate roof	1		
	109	2		
	111	1		
	241 Beacon Terrace	1		
	239	1		
	vacant lot			
	231	1		
	no buildings on alley	—		

Form S220 (rev. 4-75)   Sheet **1** of **1**

Illustration 10-14b
COMPLETED BUILDING LISTING FOR A THREE PART CHUNK

BUILDING LISTING SHEET

Primary Area: **Henley, Nev.**
Location: **Carsonville**
Chunk: **6003**
Estimated HUS: **38**
Census Tract: _____
Census Block: _____

Survey Research Center
The University of Michigan
Date: **Sept. 20, 1973**
Lister: **Doris Darrah**

(A) II	(B) Address and/or Description (specify street number; street, avenue, or boulevard, etc.; and whether north or south, etc.)	(C) Approx. No. of HUS	(D)	(E)
	236 Beacon Terrace	1		
	238	1		
	240	1		
	242	1		
	115 Floyd St.	1		
	117	1		
	119	1		
	125	1		
	127	1		
	129	1		
	135	1		
	137	1		
	141 Pizza Palace	0		
	Kit Carson Elementary School	0		
	and playground take up entire	—		
	side of block on Middlesex	—		
	no buildings on alley	—		

Form S220 (rev. 4-75)   Sheet 1 of 1

Illustration 10-14c
COMPLETED BUILDING LISTING FOR A THREE PART CHUNK

BUILDING LISTING SHEET

Primary Area: **Henley, Nev.**
Location: **Carsonville**
Chunk: **6003**
Estimated HUS: **38**
Census Tract: _____
Census Block: _____

Survey Research Center
The University of Michigan
Date: **Sept. 20, 1973**
Lister: **Doris Darrah**

(A)	(B) Address and/or Description (specify street number; street, avenue, or boulevard, etc.; and whether north or south, etc.)	(C) Approx. No. of HUS	(D)	(E)
III	208 Church Street – 1st Baptist Church	0		
	no buildings on alley	—		
	221 Middlesex Drive	1		
	211	1		
	201 Professional Offices – Dr. King	0		
	146 Pioneer Street	1		
	142	1		
	138	1		
	Apt. over garage behind 138	1		
	134	1		
	130	1		
	126	1		
	122	1		
	118	1		
	114	1		
	Parking lot for church	0		

Form S220 (rev. 4-75) Sheet 1 of 1

manufacturing plants, since the residential development of such lots is unlikely, but *do* note independent lots, since parking may be only a temporary use pending other development of the land.

- Playgrounds, parks.
- Golf courses.
- Open storage or junk yards.
- Garbage dumps, sanitary landfills.
- Sand and gravel pits, quarries, or strip mines.
- Cemeteries.
- Land unsuitable for future development because of river flood plains, extremely steep slopes, or bluffs.

In short, add information to the listing sheet just as you do to the chunk sketch when you are using the area procedure so that we will have as clear an idea as possible of what the chunk looks like.

Complete Information Sheet for Chunk

Add up the estimated number of HU's in column C and complete the Information Sheet just as you would for the area procedure. (See page 50 in this chapter.)

Return Materials to Ann Arbor

When you have completed the building listing, return the following materials to the Ann Arbor office:

- The Field Map.
- The Building Listing Sheets and chunk sketch, if any.
- The completed Information Sheet.
- Any additional notes, sketches, enlargements, etc., that you feel would be useful to describe the chunk.

11 LISTING AND UPDATING DURING THE INTERVIEWING PERIOD

In surveys of approximately 1,500 interviews, each sample housing unit represents about 30,000 HU's, so that if even one is omitted, the consequences are serious. The accuracy of our survey estimates depends on the accuracy of the interviewers' listings.

MATERIALS

Use the following materials for listing both area and building segments:
- Map for each sample location (county or town map).
- Blue Folder for each chunk in which you are to interview.
- Yellow Folder (duplicate of the Blue Folder).
- Segment Listing Sheets (Forms S210).
- Sample Address Summary Forms.
- Cover sheets.

Maps for Sample Locations Maps for each sample location are sent to the field when a chunk is first used on a study. These maps identify the new chunks, and are to be kept in the field for use on future studies.

Blue Folders The Blue Folder is a complete and continuing record for one chunk. It is used to indicate the addresses at which you are to attempt interviews.

Cover The Blue Folder cover (Illustrations 11-1 and 11-7) identifies segments selected for interviewing on a study and includes the following information:

- *Primary area name* — in the top left hand corner.
- *Sample location name* — on the line just below the primary area name. An area may be known locally by a name other than the one listed here. For example, the residents may have voted to change the name, or annexations may have put part of a sample location within the boundaries of an adjacent city. Do not worry about this or attempt to correct the sample location name, as it is used for identification on our sampling records.
- *Chunk number* — a numerical identification assigned in the Ann Arbor office; only one chunk appears in each Blue Folder.
- *Post Office and ZIP codes* — you are to provide this information for the purpose of sending respondent letters if the study requires them.
- A *segment number* (column 1) which consists of four digits (the chunk number) and a letter (the segment designation); e.g., "6003A" identifies chunk 6003 segment A. Segment numbers are listed in column 1 on the Blue Folder cover in the order in which they were selected for interviewing, and *not* necessarily in alphabetical order (Illustration 11-1).

INTERVIEWER'S MANUAL

- A *project number* (column 2) designates the study for which a segment has been selected. More than one segment in a chunk may be used on a particular study.

- The *month and year* in which a segment is used on a study are entered in column 3.

- Segments are identified as *"take-all"* or *"take-part"* by an "X" in the appropriate place in column 4. *All* housing units within a take-all segment are to be included in the study.

  Some segments contain more housing units than we wish to use on one study. These will be designated as "take-part," and only specified fractions of the HU's located within these segments are to be included on any one study. The number for a take-part segment is entered in column 1 *each time* such a segment is selected for interviewing; see the two entries of Segment 6003A in column 1 (Illustration 11-1). This segment has been used on two projects. The numbers in column 5 designate the *listing sheet numbers in take-part segments* which are to be included on a particular study. These line numbers are covered with black tape and are not to be uncovered until the listing of the segment is completed. If the segment has been listed on a previous study, black tape will not be used. It is used as an aid in preventing unconscious bias in the listing pattern because of previous knowledge of which lines will fall into the sample.

- Space is provided for any brief *comments* or *instructions* (column 6) which we wish to give concerning a segment.

Inside Spine — Inside the spine of the newest Blue Folders is an alphabetical index. Use this to check off segments as they are listed and clipped inside the folder. This will serve as a quick reference as to which segments have been previously listed (Illustration 11-5).

Back Cover — The back cover defines typical roof lines and chimneys. These terms may be useful when you are selecting permanent features for descriptive listings (Illustration 11-6).

Contents For Area Segments — A sketch of the chunk is taped inside the Blue Folder. On the sketch, the chunk is identified by number and outlined in red; segments are outlined in blue and identified by letters (Illustration 11-2a). A clip is provided on the inside of the back cover for attaching Segment Listing Sheets.

Contents For Building Segments — The original Building Listing Sheets for the chunk, with a chunk sketch at the top of the first sheet or attached underneath, are fastened inside the Blue Folder cover (Illustration 11-8). The segments are bracketed in green at the left side (column A) of the Building Listing Sheet and each segment is identified by a unique letter in column A outside the bracket. The selected segment(s) for each study is/are identified by the project number below the segment letter(s) on the Building Listing Sheet. For discussion purposes, we have treated the chunk 6003 as an area segment in Illustrations 11-1 through 11-4, and as a building segment in Illustrations 11-7, 11-8, and 11-9. Since there are clear street names and addresses in this chunk, you would normally have chosen the building listing procedure when scouting the chunk.

Yellow Folders — *The first time a chunk is used on a study,* the Field Coordinator is sent both a Yellow Folder and a Blue Folder. The Yellow Folder is a field copy and is intended to be an *exact duplicate of the Blue Folder*. It is to contain duplicate sketch maps and copies of the Segment Listing

Illustration 11-1
BLUE FOLDER COVER — AREA SEGMENT

PRIMARY ~~PSU AREA~~ AREA: Henley, Nev.   OFFICE COPY   Post Office: Carsonville
Sample Location: Carsonville   Zip Code: 89701
Chunk No. 6003

Form S200 (Rev. 7-74)

SEGMENT CONTROL RECORD

Segment No.	Project No.	Date	Take All	Take Part	If Take Part, Sample Line Numbers	Comments
1	2	3	4		5	6
6003A	454923	MARCH '74		X	2, 5, 8, 11, 14, 17, 20, 23, 26, 29, 32, 35	MAR 23 1974
6003A	467653	SEPT '74		X	1, 4, 7, 10, 13, 16, 19, 22, 25, 28, 31, 34	
6003B	467653	SEPT '74	X			

Property of
SURVEY RESEARCH CENTER
The University of Michigan

Illustration 11-2
CHUNK SKETCH — AREA SEGMENT

Primary Area: Henley Nev
Sample Location: Carsonville
Chunk: 6003

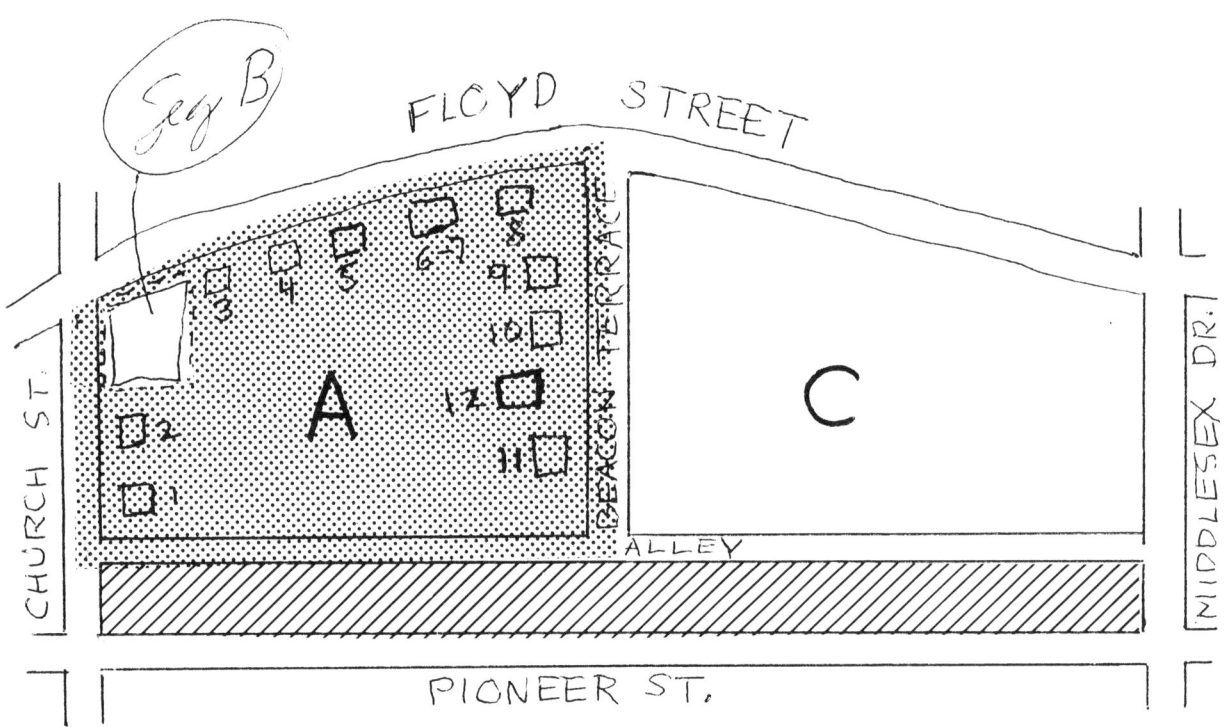

Segment B is defined as entire structure numbered 240, 242 Church St. and 101 Floyd St.

Illustration 11-3
SEGMENT LISTING 6003B — TAKE-ALL SEGMENT

SURVEY RESEARCH CENTER

SEGMENT LISTING SHEET

A. LISTED BY **L. McCleary** DATE **9/74**
B. UPDATED BY _____ DATE _____
_____ DATE _____

C. PRIMARY AREA **Henley, Nev.**
LOCATION **Carsonville**
D. SEGMENT NO. **6003B**
E. TYPE OF SEGMENT:
Take-all ☒
Take-part ☐

Line No.	Address (or description) of Housing Unit	Project Number(s)
1.	240 Church Street	467653
2.	101 Floyd Street Apt. A	467653
3.	101 Apt. B	467653
4.	101 Apt. C	467653
5.		
6.		
7.		
8.		
9.		
0.		

Form S210 (1975)   SHEET **1** OF **1** SHEETS

Illustration 11-4
SEGMENT LISTING 6003A — TAKE-PART SEGMENT

SRC SURVEY RESEARCH CENTER

SEGMENT LISTING SHEET

A. LISTED BY _Doris Darrah_ DATE _Mar. '74_
B. UPDATED BY _L. McCleary_ DATE _9/74_
_____ DATE _____

C. PRIMARY AREA _Henley, Nev._
   LOCATION _Carsonville_
D. SEGMENT NO. _6003 A_
E. TYPE OF SEGMENT:
   Take-all ☐
   Take-part ☒

Line No.	Address (or description) of Housing Unit	Project Number(s)
1.	236 Church Street	467653
2.	238 ↓	454923
3.	103 Floyd Street	
4.	105	467653
5.	(107) Single story, tan brick, green slate roof	454923
6.	109 first floor	
7.	109 second floor	467653
8.	111 ↓	
9.	241 Beacon Terrace	
10.	239 ↓	

Form S210 (1975)　　　　SHEET _1_ OF _2_ SHEETS

Illustration 11-4 (continued)

SRC SURVEY RESEARCH CENTER

SEGMENT LISTING SHEET

A. LISTED BY *Doris Darrah* DATE *Mar. 74*
B. UPDATED BY *L. McCleary* DATE *9/74*
_____ DATE _____

C. PRIMARY AREA *Henley, Nev.*
   LOCATION *Carsonville*
D. SEGMENT NO. *6003A*
E. TYPE OF SEGMENT:
   Take-all ☐
   Take-part ☒

Line No.	Address (or description) of Housing Unit	Project Number(s)
	(Line 12 belongs here)	
1.	231 Beacon Terrace	454923
March 1st JM		
2.	235 Beacon Terrace (under construction) 9/12/74	
3.		
4.		
5.		
6.		
7.		
8.		
9.		
0.		

Form S210 (1975)   SHEET *2* OF *2* SHEETS

Illustration 11-5
INSIDE SPINE AND BACK COVER OF BLUE FOLDER

LISTED SEGMENTS

- ~~A~~
- ~~B~~
- C
- D
- E
- F
- G
- H
- I
- J
- K
- L
- M
- N
- O
- P
- Q
- R
- S
- T
- U
- V
- W
- X
- Y
- Z

CROSS OFF AS LISTING FILED. NEVER RELIST!

City: Henley, Nev.
Primary Area.

Sample Location: Carsonville

Chunk No. 6003

Illustration 11-6
BACK OF BLUE FOLDER

ROOF TYPES

LOW GABLE

CROSS GABLE

HIPPED CROSS GABLE

MEDIUM GABLE

PYRAMID

BELLCAST GABLE

HIGH GABLE

HIP

GAMBREL

STEPPED OR CROWSTEPPED GABLES

HIPPED GABLE

MANSARD OR CURB

CENTER GABLE

DECK

DORMERS

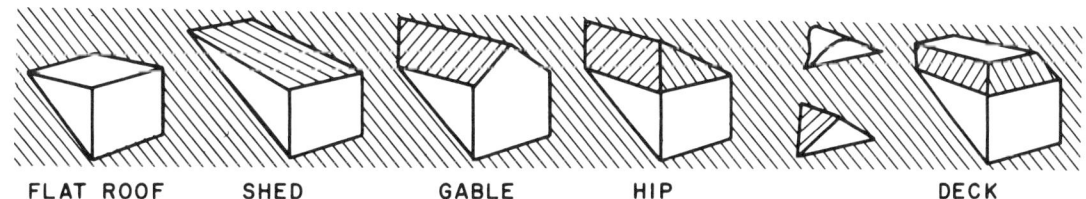

FLAT ROOF   SHED   GABLE   HIP   DECK

CHIMNEYS

INSIDE END

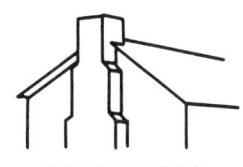
OUTSIDE END

CENTRAL

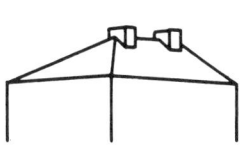
INTERIOR

Illustration 11-7
BLUE FOLDER COVER — BUILDING SEGMENT

Primary ~~PSU~~ Area: Henley, Nev.
Sample Location: Carsonville
OFFICE COPY
Post Office: Carsonville
Zip Code: 89701
Chunk No. 6003

Form S200 (Rev. 7-74)

SEGMENT CONTROL RECORD

Segment No.	Project No.	Date	Check One — Take All	Check One — Take Part	If Take Part, Sample Line Numbers	Comments
1	2	3	4	4	5	6
6003 E	454900	Feb, '74		X	2, 4, 6, 8, 10, 12, 14, 16, 18, 20, 22, 24	

Property of
SURVEY RESEARCH CENTER
The University of Michigan

Illustration 11-8
BUILDING LISTING SHEET FOR PART ONE OF CHUNK 6003

BUILDING LISTING SHEET

Primary Area: **Henley, Nev.**
Location: **Carsonville**
Chunk: **6003**
Estimated HUS: **38**
Census Tract: _____
Census Block: _____

Survey Research Center
The University of Michigan
Date: **Sept. 20, 1973**
Lister: **Doris Darrah**

(A)	(B) Address and/or Description (specify street number; street, avenue, or boulevard, etc.; and whether north or south, etc.)	(C) Approx. No. of HUS	(D)	(E)
I				
	232 Church St — Golden Standard Station	0		
	234 — L & L Grocery	0		
	236	1		
E	238	1		
	240 — storefront converted to apartment — commercial building with upstairs apts enter off Floyd St.	1		
	242 — Nugget Cleaners	0		
	101 Floyd St.	3		
	103	1		
F	105	1		
	Brown brick, 1 story, slate roof	1		
	109	2		
	111	1		
	241 Beacon Terrace	1		
G	239	1		
	vacant lot			
	231	1		
	no buildings on alley	—		
	next listed address is 232 Church St.			

Form S220 (rev. 4-75)   Sheet 1 of 1

Illustration 11-9
SEGMENT LISTING 6003E — TAKE-PART SEGMENT

SURVEY RESEARCH CENTER

SEGMENT LISTING SHEET

A. LISTED BY _Doris Darrah_ DATE _2/8/74_
B. UPDATED BY _____ DATE _____
_____ DATE _____

C. PRIMARY AREA _Henley, Nev._
   LOCATION _Carsonville_
D. SEGMENT NO. _6003 E_
E. TYPE OF SEGMENT:
   Take-all ☐
   Take-part ☒

Line No.	Address (or description) of Housing Unit			Project Number(s)
1.	236	Church Street		
2.	238	↓		454900
3.	240	↓		
4.	101	Floyd Street	Apt. A	454900
5.	101	↓	Apt. B	
6.	101	↓	Apt. C	454900
7.				
8.				
9.				
0.				

Form S210 (1975)

SHEET _1_ OF _1_ SHEETS

Listing and Updating

Sheets, and is to be kept in the primary area files when it is not in use. For each study, entries on the cover of the Blue Folder are to be copied onto the cover of the Yellow Folder. You will use the Yellow Folder after you return the Blue Folder to the Ann Arbor office.

Segment Listing Sheets

At the top of these forms (Illustrations 11-3, 11-4, and 11-9), lettered spaces A and B are to be completed by the person doing the listing. This will enable the office to contact the person who did the listing in case additional information is needed. Items C, D, and E are completed by the Ann Arbor office before the segment is sent out to be listed.

Line numbers are printed on listing sheets as 1-9 and then 0. Add 1 to the left of the 0 to form 10; on subsequent sheets, add 1, 2, 3, etc. to the left of the printed number to create line numbers 11-20, 21-30, and so on.

As lines are designated for a project on the Blue Folder cover, write the project number in the project number column of the Segment Listing Sheet.

Segment Listing Sheets are prepared in copy sets. *The original is to be placed in the Blue Folder and the carbon copy in the Yellow Folder.*

Sample Address Summary Forms

Sample Address Summary Forms (Illustration 11-11) come in copy sets containing a green form and a sturdy cream-colored sheet. These forms also come as single white sheets.

Cover Sheets

Prepare a cover sheet for each Segment Listing Sheet line in the sample; there must be an accounting for all sample listings. Enter only the identifying information on the cover sheet before you call at a sample address. Other items are to be completed at the time of interviewing. (See Chapter 12.)

PROCEDURES FOR LISTING IN SAMPLE SEGMENTS

When you are listing in segments your job is to:
- Check the segment boundaries.
- Check notations in the Blue Folder and locate the original listing if the segment was used before.
- List on foot in the segment.
- List all HU's and only HU's on the Segment Listing Sheet, one HU per line.
- Record a unique identification for each HU.
- Identify HU's in multi-unit buildings, making inquiries when they are necessary.

Check Segment Boundaries

Before you start listing in a sample segment, verify that you have located the boundaries, as described on the map and in the Blue Folder; otherwise some HU's in the segment might be omitted, and HU's outside the segment might be included.

Area Segments Defined

Area segments are identified by letter on the chunk sketch. Exact boundaries are outlined in blue, and each segment is shaded in some color to distinguish it from adjacent segments. An area segment includes all of the geographical area and all of the HU's within its boundaries, as shown on the chunk sketch (Illustration 11-2).

Building Segments Defined

Building segments are bracketed in green and identified by letter on the Building Listing Sheet. A building segment includes all HU's beginning with the first address or description inside the bracket and continuing *beyond* the bracket and up to but *not including* the address or description recorded on the succeeding line (following the bracket) of the Building Listing Sheet. Note that the listed address or description succeeding the *last* segment in a block is the first listed address or description in the block.

In Illustration 11-8, segment E begins with 232 Church St. and includes all HU's within the area from 232 Church St. *up to* 103 Floyd St.; 103 Floyd St. is part of segment F. Segment G, the last segment in block I, begins with 109 Floyd St. and continues up to (but does not include) 232 Church St., the first listed address in the block. Any residential building missing from the Building Listing Sheet is still associated with *one* of the building segments, so that HU's in a missed building have a chance to become sample HU's.

Check Notations in Blue Folder

To be sure that the segment has not been listed on a previous study, look at the notations on the Blue Folder cover, the headings on Segment Listing Sheets already inside the Blue Folder, and the checklist on the inside spine of the Blue Folder. *NEVER RELIST.* If a segment has been listed on a previous study, follow the instructions for updating and perfecting the listing on pages 86 through 90.

List on Foot in the Segment

Go to the segment to do the listing. The building listings may be out-of-date so that you must prepare a current, on-the-site listing of HU's. DO NOT copy a segment listing from a building listing.

Listing is best done on foot, unless you must cover great distances or there are other extenuating circumstances. If you try to list from a car, you will miss obscure HU's, and house numbers and other distinguishing features are harder to see.

List ALL HU's and ONLY HU's

It is essential that all HU's in the segment be listed. This means you must use a systematic approach. In area segments select a specific starting point and proceed to cover the segments in clockwise order. In building segments follow the order of listing that you find on the Building Listing Sheet. Start with the first entry for the selected segment and continue up to the first listing of the following segment. List systematically, recording the address, or description and location if there is no street address, of each HU in the segment. You, or any other interviewer, should be able to locate *any* HU in the segment by using the listing sheet.

List on the Segment Listing Sheet

As you list, record the HU addresses or descriptions on the Segment Listing Sheet (Illustration 11-3, Form S210) as neatly as possible. Do not rewrite or type the listing after you return home. Many errors have been made during well-intentioned transfers of HU's from the listing sheet prepared in the field to a new listing form at home.

List Each HU on a Separate Line

Use one and only one line for listing each HU. In a multi-unit structure, for example, list each apartment on a separate line of the Segment Listing Sheet.

Record Unique Identification for Each HU

Unique identification may be more than just a street name and number: "109 Floyd St., First Floor" distinguishes an HU separate from "109 Floyd St., Second Floor." If you cannot ascertain the location of an HU in a structure, *do not guess*. A unique identification always includes street name and a full address or description.

Street, Road, or Highway on which the HU is Located

Use *complete* street names including "Street" or "Place" or "Boulevard," "North," "South," etc. Since street signs often give only the name and do not specify "Avenue," "Street," "North," etc., you may have to get this information from a map, a ZIP code directory, or some other source.

Listing and Updating

House or
Building Number

If this cannot be ascertained, give a description of the building. Do not attempt to guess the number from the sequence of numbers you have observed. If no number is visible, inquire or describe the HU.

Description of
Unnumbered Residential
Buildings

Sometimes the best description is a building's location; e.g., "house between 28 and 34 Oak St." Do not depend on numbers on roadside mail boxes, since the boxes may be for houses across the street from the segment.

Choose features which will distinguish that house from all others in the neighborhood, when describing a residential building for which there is no number. *Good descriptive features* are type and construction of house and roof; e.g., two-story, brick, central chimney, attached garage; or, single-story frame with field stone foundation, low gable roof. Other good descriptive features are those which are relatively permanent, such as the position of doors, chimneys, garages and other buildings, distance back from the road, and so forth. Roof and chimney types are illustrated and labeled on the back of the Blue Folder to aid you in describing permanent features (Illustration 11-6). Other less helpful descriptive features include landscaping and vegetation (hedge in front, two large maples in the side yard) and other such semi-permanent features as flagstone walks, picket fences, fire numbers on utility poles, and roof color or composition. Descriptive features such as the color of the house or trim, lawn ornaments, and children's swing sets are of little help.

Identification of HU's
in a Multi-Unit
Building

When you can see from outside that a building contains more than one HU, list each HU separately in an orderly fashion. A unique identification of these HU's requires an apartment number, letter, or description locating the HU within the building. *Inquire about the number of HU's and specifically identify each HU in every multi-unit building.* If an HU does not have an apartment number or letter, give the location inside the building, or even better, the location of the door which would normally be used by a visitor at the HU (Illustration 11-10). Sometimes these are fairly obvious; if they are not, you might consult the manager or some other responsible person regarding the number and location of HU's in the building. When this is impractical, determine as best you can the number of HU's and list the building address on the number of lines corresponding to that number. When you start to interview, inquire about the specific location of all HU's within the building and complete your listing by entering a description (First Floor left, etc.) on each line after the street address.

When making inquiries, do not use the term "housing unit"; this is a technical term for which we have a specific definition, which is not readily understood by the public. Instead, it may be helpful to ask questions such as: Is this a single-family house? Are there apartments? Are there lodgers? How many? Other useful questions may be derived from the definition of an HU in Chapter 9.

Listing HU's in a multi-unit structure requires some systematic procedure to ensure that each HU is listed once and only once. One or a combination of the following rules will satisfy most situations:

- List by number or by letter.
- List by floors, from basement to attic.
- If there are several unnumbered units on a floor, begin at the front left as you face the building and list systematically in a clockwise direction.
- If necessary, draw a rough floor plan to show the locations of unnumbered units.

Illustration 11-10
SEVERAL HU'S IN A BUILDING AND THE SEQUENCE OF LISTING

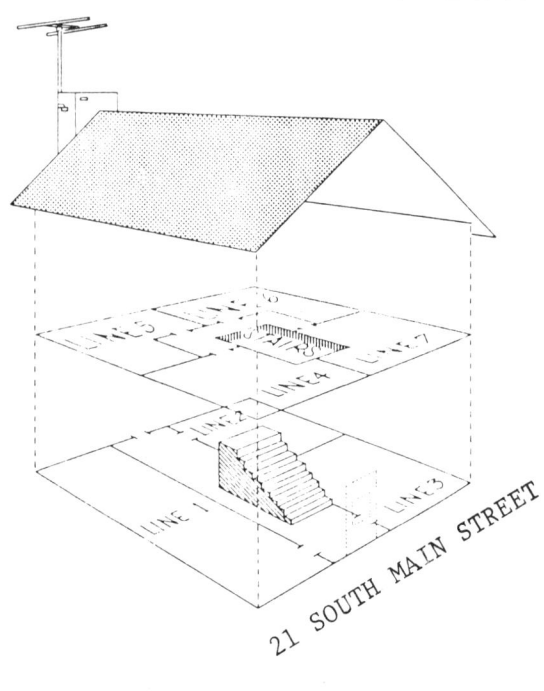

1.	21 S. Main, first floor left
2.	" 1st fl. right rear
3.	" 1st fl. right front
4.	" 2nd fl. left front
5.	" 2nd fl. left rear
6.	" 2nd fl. right rear
7.	" 2nd fl. right front
8.	
9.	
0.	

TYPES OF LIVING QUARTERS

The majority of HU's are single-family houses. However, you should be familiar with all types of housing and the procedures for handling them.

Single-Family Houses

There should be few problems involved in listing single-family houses. This does not mean, however, that listing what appear to be single-family houses is always a simple and straightforward task. It is easy to overlook extra apartments in attics or basements, houses along alleys, HU's over garages, etc.

Row Houses, Town Houses, Terrace, or Garden Apartment Developments

In apartment developments consisting of buildings such as row houses, town houses, village, terrace, and garden-type apartments, list each HU on a separate line of the listing form.

Small Multi-unit Buildings

Even though a structure might appear to be a single-family house, be on the lookout for evidence of more than one HU in a structure, such as an extra apartment in the attic or basement, or a rear dwelling. There are a number of clues to look for in order to determine if a single structure contains more than one HU. For example: several mailboxes or doorbells; more than one gas or electric meter; more garbage cans than a single HU would be likely to require; more than one main entrance to the structure; more than one TV antenna on the roof. Look for special quarters (such as a custodian's) that have entrances on the side or the back of the building.

Regular Apartment Buildings

You will rarely be asked to list more than one floor of an apartment building, but the listing should always be systematic. (See "Identification of HU's in a Multi-Unit Building," page 79.)

Listing and Updating

Segments That are Parts of Buildings

Usually you will have no difficulty locating segments that are parts of buildings. The description(s) will clearly specify what is to be included; e.g., "Segment 1002F consists of the basement, 1st, and 2nd floors of 348 34th St."

Please note that in some segment descriptions, the basement will be combined with one or more of the lower floors; the upper floors are indicated by the notation "and above," when the last floor of a building is part of a segment. This accounts for the total area of an apartment building at the time of the original field work and encompasses future building changes which can occur during the life of the segment.

Trailers, Trailer Courts or Parks

Review the definitions of transient or seasonal units in the section "Definition of Excluded Quarters," Chapter 9. If a trailer court or park is nontransient and nonseasonal, *list each established space, whether or not it is currently occupied by a trailer*. Trailer parks usually have specified spaces with electric and sewage facilities at definite locations.

If a trailer court or park is transient and/or seasonal, list any manager's or custodian's quarters that you find.

All residential trailers with permanent foundations or permanent electric and sewage tie-ins are to be listed, whether or not they are occupied. Trailers which do not meet these criteria are to be listed only if they are occupied.

HU's in Buildings Used for Nonresidential Purposes

Even if a building appears to be strictly commercial, it may contain HU's above or behind shops and stores; the storekeepers may have their living quarters in such places, or extra space may have been converted into apartments. In churches, private schools, etc., there may be living quarters for janitors or maintenance men. Occasionally manufacturing or warehouse structures will contain quarters for watchmen. List all such quarters if they meet the definition of an HU.

Temporary Nonresidential Use of HU's

Dwellings are sometimes used *temporarily* for other purposes such as professional offices or storage, and you are to list these units. Quarters hich have been permanently converted for some other use, of course, are no longer HU's.

Vacant or Dilapidated HU's

The general rule is to list vacant HU's. If there are several in the same building, list each one separately. The rules for listing vacant living quarters are similar to those for listing occupied quarters.

If a vacant unit is unfit for human habitation and no longer considered as living quarters, do not list it. If you question whether or not a vacant unit is fit for habitation, list it.

Do not list HU's which are scheduled for demolition. Such places are usually located in urban redevelopment areas or along highways under construction. Please describe what (if anything) is planned to take the place of the structures to be demolished. If there will be more residential units — such as housing projects or high-rise apartment buildings — get full details.

HU's Under Construction

List unfinished residential buildings on which *any* construction has been started. For multi-unit buildings, list each HU which the building will contain when it is completed, and estimate the completion date. Describe the location of each unit. If this information cannot be obtained at the building site, try to locate the builder, contractor, or some other local source in order to secure the information.

INTERVIEWER'S MANUAL

Hotels and Motels

In general, we wish to include permanent residents living in hotels, and to exclude the transient population. If your segment includes a hotel or motel:

- Refer to the section on "Definition of Excluded Quarters," Chapter 9, and review the definitions of transient and seasonal quarters. Do not list living quarters that we would classify as transient or seasonal, but in excluded quarters, *do list HU's occupied by resident managers or staff.*

- For nontransient or nonseasonal hotels or motels, do list each unit that meets the HU definition.

Rooming Houses

For rooming houses with living quarters that meet the HU definition, list each HU on a separate line of the listing sheet. Be sure to include the landlord's quarters. In rare cases, the separate rooms in a rooming house will not fit the definition of an HU. Look for the landlord's apartment, however, and list it. Note on the listing sheet line for the landlord's quarters that it is a rooming house. If there is no landlord's apartment or HU, define the house as one HU and list it on one line of the listing sheet.

Seasonal Housing

Review the definition of "Transient or Seasonal" housing (Chapter 9, p. 40) for seasonal areas. If you determine that scattered lake cottages, hunting lodges, migratory labor housing, and similar units meet the HU definition, list each unit on a separate line of the listing form. In addition, enter an "S" to the left of the line number for each such unit.

Military Reservations

We do not include military reservations in our sample surveys, and, even though there are HU's for civilian personnel on military bases, you are not to list them. Veterans' hospitals, however, are not considered military bases and should be checked for HU's occupied by staff or other employees.

Institutional Quarters

Do not list institutional quarters which are occupied or intended for occupancy by the persons for whom the facility is operated.

The types of institutional quarters to be excluded are described on page 40 of Chapter 9.

Remember to check carefully for HU's within institutional grounds. The following examples should make this clear.

TYPE OF INSTITUTION	LOOK FOR AND LIST HU'S FOR:
Hospitals	Nurses, interns, or dieticians
Mental or penal institutions	Superintendents, wardens, guards, and attendants
Rest or nursing homes	Owners or managers
Dormitories, fraternities, and sororities	Resident staff
YMCA's, residential clubs	Directors, permanent residents
Missions, flophouses, Salvation Army shelters	Superintendents, directors, janitors

GUIDELINES FOR LISTING

HOUSING UNITS	INSTRUCTIONS
— Single family houses, apartments, mobile homes, etc.	List each HU
— Trailers in nonexcluded trailer courts	List each trailer *space*
— Vacant HU's:	
• sound condition	List each HU
• deteriorated (appears habitable with minor or moderate repair)	List each HU
• dilapidated (repair costs clearly preclude future human habitation)	Do not list
• vacant and scheduled for demolition (regardless of condition)	Do not list; send memo with Blue Folder describing what will replace it
— Building under construction	List each intended HU within building under construction
— Former HU now in nonresidential use	List if temporarily for other use; if permanently converted for other use, do not list
— Student housing that qualifies as HU's	List each HU

EXCLUDED QUARTERS	INSTRUCTIONS
— Quarters for persons for whom institution is operated	Do not list
— Quarters in facilities which meet the transient or seasonal definition	List manager's or staff's quarters only

UNCLASSIFIED QUARTERS	INSTRUCTIONS
— Living quarters that neither clearly meet the HU criteria nor are clearly to be excluded	Check with the Ann Arbor office

COMPLETING SAMPLING FORMS

After the segments have been listed, complete the job as described below.

Enter Project Numbers on Assigned Lines

When the listing (or updating) is completed, refer to columns 4 and 5 on the Blue Folder cover to determine the assigned line numbers (Illustrations 11-1 and 11-7). For a take-part segment which is being used for the first time, remove the black tape on the Blue Folder cover. Then, in the right hand column of the listing sheet, write the project number on each *selected* line with an HU address or description (Illustrations 11-4 and 11-9). For a take-all segment, write the project number on *each* line with an HU address or description (Illustration 11-3).

Identify Oversized Segments

If there are 13 or more HU's listed in a take-all segment, then it is oversized. In a take-part segment, if the last listed line number on the Segment Listing Sheet is greater than the last line number shown in column 5 of the Blue Folder cover, the segment is oversized. Send us a complete listing of the oversized segment at once, along with a sketch of the area showing the locations of all HU's and a description of the situation. Do not conduct any interviews in the oversized segment, but go ahead in your other segments.

If a segment has more than 10 HU's, you will need to use an additional set of listing forms to complete the segment. Be sure to complete all heading information and line numbers on the additional set(s). At the

INTERVIEWER'S MANUAL

bottom right of the listing form there are spaces which you can fill in to indicate the number and sequence of the listing sheets you use to list the segment.

Put Listing Sheet in Blue Folder

After you have listed all the HU's in a segment and checked for oversized segments, put the original copy of the listing sheet in the Blue Folder and the carbon copy in the Yellow Folder.

Make Out Sample Address Summary Forms

After you have listed (or updated) the selected segments, make out Sample Address Summary Forms. *Use one form for each segment.* Return the sturdy cream-colored sheet with the Blue Folder to the Ann Arbor office immediately. The Field Coordinator is to retain the original (green) Sample Address Summary Form for all the addresses in the sample. Use white summary sheets to record your own assigned addresses and to keep track of your progress on each address.

Heading

In the heading record the *project number, primary area name,* and *sample location name* (Illustration 11-11).

Address

For each sample line, copy the address or description *verbatim* from the Segment Listing Sheet. Be sure that a street name or highway route number (on which the address is located) appears on each line. Enter the capital letter "L" with line number *below* it to the left of each address on the copy set.

Segment Number

In the double-ruled column to the right of the "address" column, enter the segment number as shown.

‖ 6003 ‖
‖ A ‖

Occasionally when you are interviewing, you may discover an unlisted HU. Each time you use a listing sheet line number for more than one sample HU, make out a cover sheet for each HU at the sample address line. Be sure this information is added to the interviewer's and Field Coordinator's copies of the Sample Address Summary Form. Send a yellow Immediate Action Form to the Field Office if the Blue Folder has already been returned. Keeping forms up-to-date will enable you to report progress accurately.

Make Cover Sheets For Every Selected Line

Complete cover sheets for *all selected listings,* even when the listing does not lead to an occupied HU or an interview. Complete the identification items on each cover sheet, and be sure that the address or description is identical with the unique identification of the HU on the Segment Listing Sheet and the Sample Address Summary Form. Make out a cover sheet for each sample line, even if the address (or description) is that of a vacant house, a demolished or unfinished housing unit, a structure converted to commercial use, or of a structure in any other nonresponse category specified for the study.

Return Blue Folder to the Ann Arbor Office

As soon as you have listed *all* HU's or updated the listing in the assigned segment, return the Blue Folder to Ann Arbor so that we can check for discrepancies and contact you before you have completed interviewing. Also, if a situation requires that you call or write the Field Office about the sample, it is helpful for us to look at an exact replica of the material under discussion. *The Yellow Folders are for your use during the remainder of the interviewing period.*

Interview Only at Assigned Locations

Attempt interviews *only* at locations designated by the line numbers assigned for the study.

Illustration 11-11
SAMPLE ADDRESS SUMMARY FORM

PROJ 467653
Primary Area Henley, New **Location** Carsonville

SAMPLE ADDRESS SUMMARY

ADDRESS		INTERVIEWER ASSIGNED	RESULT ON CALLS					DATE MAILED	COMMENTS
			1ST	2ND	3RD	4TH	ADD		
L 1	236 Church St.	6003 A	9/9 HV					Sept. 12	
L 4	105 Floyd St.		9/9 NOC	9/10 Apt.	9/10 Int.			Sept. 12	
L 7	109 Floyd St., 2nd floor		9/9 Int.						
L 10	239 Beacon Terrace		9/10 NOC	9/12 NOC	9/12 NOC	9/14 NOC	9/15 7:30pm Int.	Sept. 19	

INTERVIEWER'S MANUAL

PERFECTING THE SAMPLE LISTING

Even after the segments have been carefully listed, the listings must be perfected and brought up-to-date. Neighborhoods are constantly changing, and what you find when you list may be different from what you find when you return, even if it is the next day, to interview. Some unusual housing situations give no clue to the interviewer who is scouting or listing that she should inquire about the location and number of housing units within a residential building. In order to perfect the segment listing we have established procedures for adding missed HU's to the list, and for identifying elements that do not properly belong on the list so that they can be accounted for and removed from our tabulations in the office. These procedures are the same for newly listed segments as they are for take-part segments already listed on a previous study.

Procedures for Updating Segments Listed on Earlier Studies

When you are updating segments listed on earlier studies you must follow these steps:

- Find the original Segment Listing Sheet in the Blue Folder.
- Check the segment in the same order as listed.
- Add HU's covered by existing listings to that line. (See Case 1 below.)
- Add HU's in unlisted buildings (see Case 2) below the red line of the Segment Listing Sheet.
- Identify listings that do not qualify for our sample. (See Cases 3 and 4 below.)
- Transfer any notes, additions, corrections, and so on from the Blue Folder to the Yellow Folder.

Find the Original Segment Listing Sheet

Check in column 1 of the Blue Folder to determine whether or not the segment had been listed earlier. You can also check this by looking at the segment letters which have been crossed off on the inside spine of the Blue Folder. Never relist a segment which was listed on a previous study. If the segment has been listed before and you cannot find the listing clipped inside the Blue Folder, notify the Ann Arbor office immediately.

Check the Segment in the Same Order as Listed

• *Area Segments.* Start at the segment boundary preceding line 1 on the listing sheet and proceed to cover the entire segment in the order of the original listing. If new streets have been cut through or into the segment, draw them on the sketch in the Blue Folder. If you find HU's in previously unlisted buildings, use small squares and listing sheet line numbers to show the locations of these buildings on the chunk sketch. Do not be disturbed if the numbering is out of order on the sketch, and NEVER RELIST.

• *Building Segments.* Refer to the Building List Sheet to establish the beginning and end point of the segment. (See page 77, "Building Segment Defined".) The order of the Building Listing always determines the line of travel. If you encounter an unlisted cul-de-sac, check it out at the point it intersects the line of travel. However, if you encounter a street or alley which bisects the block and which has not been covered on the Building Listing Sheet, you will need to draw a rough sketch of the area, showing the new street(s) or alley(s). On a separate piece of paper, list HU's on these newly discovered streets which divide the block and send this information to the Ann Arbor office. If there are any HU's on these streets, do not interview in the segment until you have received instructions.

Listing and Updating

If you find HU's that do not appear on the S210 (Segment Listing Sheet), enter them according to the rules presented in Cases 1 and 2 below. Make these entries only on the Segment Listing Sheet; do NOT enter them on the Building Listing Sheet.

In order to add HU's which were missed to the listing, you must first determine whether or not the previously unlisted HU's you find are covered by existing lines. If they are covered by a listed line, add them to that line; if they are not covered, list them on the first available line. The following cases illustrate this distinction.

Add HU's Covered by Existing Listings to that Line

- **CASE 1:** *A line on the Segment Listing Sheet identifies more than one HU.* (See lines 1, 3, 4, and 5 of Illustration 11-12.)

If the total number of HU's covered by any one segment listing line is four or fewer, add the unique identification for each HU to the listing sheet line. When that line is selected for a study, make out a cover sheet with that unique identification for each HU covered by the listing. When making out cover sheets for the additional HU's, *use the same line number* as that of the originally listed HU.

If there are five or more HU's covered by the same line (the originally listed HU plus four or more previously unlisted ones), notify the Ann Arbor office immediately and await instructions before making out additional cover sheets or interviewing at that listing.

Add HU's in Unlisted Buildings Below the Red Line on the Segment Listing Sheet

- **CASE 2:** *One or more HU's within the segment are not identified on any listing line.* (See lines 2, and 6 through 12 of Illustration 11-12.)

If there are HU's within the segment which are not identified or covered by any listed line, record the addresses or unique identification for these on the Segment Listing Sheet, one HU per line, beginning with the first available line. Make a marginal note on the listing sheet at the place where the unlisted HU would be located in the original listing sequence. (See note on line 11 of Illustration 11-4.) NEVER RELIST.

If you find enough new HU's to make the total segment oversized (see page 83, "Identify Oversized Segments"), report the situation to the Ann Arbor office and do not interview until you receive instructions. Your report should include a sketch showing the locations of the newly found HU's and a listing of them on a separate sheet. If a new subdivision or apartment complex has been built in the segment, try to get a plat map or site plan of the development.

Identify Listings That Do Not Qualify For Our Samples

When you are updating, you may discover that the listing identifies something that does not qualify for our sample. A detailed discussion of the reasons a listing may not qualify is presented in Chapter 12. (See page 97, "NONRESPONSE CLASSIFICATION".) Procedures for handling situations you are likely to encounter during updating are presented in Cases 3 and 4 below.

- **CASE 3:** *The Listing Describes Something Which Is Not An HU.* If a line on the Segment Listing Sheet identifies something which is not presently an HU (e.g., building demolished, construction not completed, used for commercial purposes), then it is considered a SLIP (Sample Listing Isn't Proper). Make out a cover sheet, check the SLIP nonresponse category, and include an explanation. (See lines 2, 3, 4, 6, and 7 on Illustration 11-13 and line 13 on Illustration 11-12.) Vacant trailer spaces *in trailer parks* are considered VTS (Vacant Trailer Space) rather than a SLIP.

Illustration 11-12
EXAMPLES OF SITUATIONS WHICH REQUIRE ADDING HU'S TO THE SEGMENT LISTING SHEET

ORIGINAL SEGMENT LISTING		WHAT YOU FIND	WHAT TO DO
			1. Add to the original line.
Line	Address or Description		2. List at the bottom, beginning on the first unused line.
1	31 Oak St.	An unnumbered side entrance, which leads to a second HU at 31 Oak St.	1
2	33 Oak St.	A side entrance, bearing the number 33½ Oak St., which leads to a second (not previously listed) HU in this building.	2
3	Large 3-story brick house, green roof, set back from road 500 ft.	2 HU's in this building	1
4	35 Oak St. first floor	2 HU's on first floor of 35 Oak St.	1
5	37 Oak St.	An unlisted apartment above an *attached* garage at 37 Oak St. No street number on garage.	1
6	39 Oak St.	An unlisted apartment above *detached* garage at 39 Oak St.	2
7-10	Listings for apartments 1-4 at 41 Oak St.	An additional apartment at this address with the designation "Apartment 5."	2
11	43 Oak St.	A separate building bearing the number 45 Oak St.	2
12	47 Oak St.		
13	49 Oak St.	The single HU described by the original listing has been demolished, and an apartment building has been erected on this site bearing the old number (49 Oak St.) and having 10 numbered units.	2 (the original 49 Oak is a SLIP)

Illustration 11-13
EXAMPLES OF LISTING PROBLEMS YOU MAY ENCOUNTER WHEN YOU CALL TO INTERVIEW

ORIGINAL SEGMENT LISTING		WHAT YOU FIND	What to Do If These Lines Are Selected For a Study
Line	Address or Description		
1	31 Oak St. first floor	The first and second floor apartments have been combined to make 1 HU	Interview at Line 1 Line 2 becomes SLIP
2	31 Oak St. 2nd floor		
3	32 Oak St.	House is outside the segment boundaries and should not have been listed.	Line 3 becomes SLIP
4	Trailer on lot between 31 & 35 Oak	New HU has been built with the number 33 Oak & trailer is now used for storage in back yard.	New HU goes on next available line. Line 4 becomes SLIP
5	35 Oak St.	The city has renumbered all HU's on Oak St. What was 35 Oak now is numbered 3017 Oak	Write new numbers beside old numbers on all listing sheets interview.
6	Trailer in back yard of 35 Oak St.	No trailer	Make out a cover sheet marked SLIP
7	37 Oak St.	This house has been converted to a doctor's office	Line 7 becomes SLIP
8	39 Oak St.	Family lives in trailer in winter— lives in 39 Oak during summer	Interview or report HV depending on where family is living
9	Trailer behind 39 Oak St.		
10	41 Oak St.	Trailer occupied by 4 sons of the family at 41 Oak	Treat 41 Oak and trailer as separate HU's. Make out cover sheets and interview at both.
11	Trailer behind 41 Oak St.		
12	Trailer space A in EZ Aces Trailer Park	No trailer on the slab	Make out a cover sheet marked VTS (Vacant Trailer Space)

INTERVIEWER'S MANUAL

• *CASE 4: The Listing Includes an HU Outside the Segment Boundaries.* If a line on the listing sheet identifies an HU outside the segment boundary (i.e., a mistake was made at the time of the original listing), and this line is selected, it is considered a SLIP. Make out a cover sheet, check the SLIP nonresponse category, and include an explanation.

Transfer Notes
and Added Listings
From Blue Folder
to Yellow Folder

When you have completed the updating process for a segment, transfer all notes, added listings, corrections, and changes in the chunk sketch from the Blue Folder to the Yellow Folder.

Interview Only
At Assigned
Locations

In segments you have updated, as in segments you have listed for the first time, interview only at those line numbers assigned for the study. Be sure you have put the project number on all sample lines.

Continue to
Perfect the
Listings as
You Interview

Take the *Yellow Folder* with you when you are interviewing in a segment so that you can continue to check the listing. In order to make sure that we do not miss any HU's that should be included, each cover sheet asks you to determine by inquiry the number of HU's at that listing line. If any of the type of HU's described in Case 1 above were missed in listing or updating, they should be picked up at this time. You may also discover some situations mentioned in Case 3 when you make calls to interview.

Wait until you begin interviewing before you decide that an HU is vacant or that it does not contain an eligible respondent. If a house was vacant when you updated a week before interviewing, it will not necessarily still be vacant when the study actually begins.

12 CHOOSING RESPONDENTS

IDENTIFYING OCCUPIED HOUSING UNITS

Before we can select a respondent, we must determine whether or not a listing describes an occupied HU. When you call to interview, you may discover that certain HU's are vacant or that the listing no longer describes an HU. For example, a listed structure may have been demolished or converted for nonresidential use.

General Rules

• *We will assume that each listing describes an occupied HU until we have information to the contrary.* If you are unable to determine from observation or inquiry that an HU is actually vacant, we will count it as occupied, even though you are unable to locate anyone at home after making repeated calls.

• *Once it is clearly established that an HU is occupied or vacant, this classification is fixed for the duration of the interviewing period.* A house which is occupied is treated as an occupied HU even if the respondent moves out before you are able to get an interview. Because study requirements vary, you are to check the study instruction book to learn what to do when respondents move. Some studies do not follow people who move after the interviewer has determined household composition. Other studies follow people only if they move within the primary area; still others will follow respondents even if they move outside of the primary area. Living quarters that are vacant are treated as "house vacant" even if a family moves in later the same day.

• *The composition of the HU is fixed at the time you are able to speak with some responsible member of the household and learn who lives there.* (Usually this is when you fill in the household listing box.) We count as members of the household all who reside there at this time, regardless of whether or not they lived there on earlier calls when you were unable to determine the composition of the household. Do not change the listing if persons move in or out of the HU between the time the household is listed and the time of interviewing. If the designated respondent moves out of the house, is hospitalized, or dies before you are able to interview him, do not select someone else unless you have specific instructions to do so.

However, if you discover that your original listing of the household was incorrect, obtain a correct listing of the household as it was at the time of the original listing, even if the corrected listing indicates that you must choose a different respondent.

Handling Difficult Cases. Occasionally you may have difficulty determining whether or not an HU is occupied. Consult apartment superintendents, mail carriers, and rental agents in order to save yourself fruitless calls. Neighbors, especially other respondents in the segment, may also be helpful. In some areas fire wardens and other local authorities often know whether or not HU's in remote areas are occupied. Because we consider an HU vacant if all the eligible people who live there are at another place of residence, you must phrase your questions carefully. Ask: "Do you know how I could get in touch with the people next door?" not "Is the house next door occupied?" The latter question is likely to arouse suspicion and lead people to provide false information in an effort to protect their neighbors.

You may need to make detailed inquiries about the living arrangements of people who are away from their usual place of residence. For example, a widow who is at her daughter's house may just be visiting, or she may have her regular summer residence there. People on an extended trip may be at their winter home in Florida, or they may be traveling about with no other place of residence. We need enough information to determine whether or not the place the people are staying would be classified as an HU; if it is an HU we also need to determine whether or not the people should be listed as residents of this other HU. If the answer to these questions is yes, consider the sample HU vacant, even if the regular occupants are expected back that afternoon.

In many cases you will not be able to get enough information to make a clear determination. In these cases, consider the HU occupied, and base any future calls on the information you have. Please record all of the information you have so that we can make a final decision if you have to send the cover sheet in as a noninterview.

INTERVIEWER'S MANUAL

Handling Seasonal Units. To minimize difficulties with vacation HU's and other seasonal units, plan your first call at such places on a regular weekday (Monday noon to Friday noon, but not on holidays). If there is no one at home and it appears as if no one will be there at night, consider the seasonal unit vacant. Consider occupied any seasonal units in which people are staying when you visit, regardless of how long they plan to stay.

NOTE: This rule on seasonal units does not apply to purely transient quarters which should not have been listed in the first place and which should be classified as SLIP (Sample Listing Isn't Proper) if they are identified as transient after listing.

SELECTING THE RESPONDENT

After you have identified a sample of occupied housing units and confirmed that they are occupied, further sampling procedures are used to select the proper respondent from among the residents of each sample HU.

For interviewing in segments, we usually use one of two procedures for selecting respondents:

- Designating the respondent by family relationship.
- Designating the respondent by a selection table.

At the beginning of each survey, you will receive instructions indicating which procedure to use. If a survey requires a selection procedure which is different from either of the two mentioned above, you will receive special instructions.

General Procedure

The general procedure in *both* cases is as follows.

Introduce Yourself

Very briefly explain why you are calling. You could mention that in order to obtain an accurate sample we need to know who is living in the household, and ask, "Could you tell me how many people live here? I don't need names — just their relationship to the head of the household."*

List HU Members

In the first column of the listing box list the head first, and then the other members of the household in whatever order they are given to you. The instruction book for each study will explain which members to list, because requirements vary from study to study.

List people according to their relationship to the head (See page 94, "Head of Family.") Please do not use names, as they do not define relationships. Use designations which indicate sex whenever possible, e.g., son or granddaughter (not child or grandchild), and wife or husband (not spouse). List persons not related to the head by position in the household: roomer, roommate, maid, housekeeper, nurse, etc. (Illustrations 12-2 and 12-3).

Be sure all residents of the HU are listed by asking, "Is there anyone else in the family?" (PAUSE) "Anyone else living here who is not related to you?" Unless you take special pains to find out about them, you are quite likely to miss roomers and unrelated persons. In larger families it is entirely possible to miss members of the family unless you check carefully. If you do not know whether or not to list persons who are temporarily present or absent, refer to the Chart for Determining Members of the Household (Illustration 12-1).

---

*"Head of household" is another term for which we have a very specific meaning, which ensures uniform listing. While people you interview will not know the specifics of our definition, the common meaning of "head of household" is close enough to enable us to ask for information in these terms. This means, however, that the interviewer must be completely familiar with our definition (see pages 94-95) so that she can skillfully and discreetly interpret what she is told and record it according to our definition. For example, if a man says, "We don't have a head here; my wife and I share all the responsibilities," don't quibble — simply list the members of the household according to their relationship to him.

Illustration 12-1
CHART FOR DETERMINING MEMBERS OF THE HOUSEHOLD

Have a place of residence here?	Have a place of residence elsewhere?	Include in household?	Examples
1. PERSONS *STAYING* IN SAMPLE UNIT AT TIME OF CONTACT.			
Yes	No	Yes	(a) Just "lives here" (b) Lodger (c) Servant
Yes	Yes	Yes*	(a) Has country home or town house. (b) Has summer home or winter home. (c) Student living here while at school, or soldier while in service. (d) Home on military leave or school recess.
No	No	Yes	(a) Waiting completion of new home. (b) Takes turns staying with children, or parents.
No	Yes	No	(a) Helping out with new baby, or during illness. (b) Visiting friends or relatives. (c) Works or eats here, sleeps elsewhere.
2. PERSONS *ABSENT* FROM SAMPLE UNIT AT TIME OF CONTACT.			
Yes	No	Yes	(a) Traveling salesman on the road. (b) Railroad man on a run. (c) In general hospital. (d) On vacation or visiting. (e) Absent on business.
Yes	Yes	No*	(a) Has country home or town house. (b) Has summer home or winter home. (c) Away at school or in service. (d) In prison or nursing home or special hospital.

3. IF "DON'T KNOW" ON ANY OF THESE CRITERIA, INCLUDE IN HOUSEHOLD.*

*Please describe situation.

INTERVIEWER'S MANUAL

Record Additional Information in the Listing Box

Record additional information in the listing box. Normally, sex will be indicated by the relationship to the head, and can be recorded as you list without additional inquiry. You may find out ages by asking, "I'd like to know the ages of the people. How old is . . . ?" (MENTION ONE.)

Requirements for Household Membership

Persons staying in the HU at the time of contact should be considered members of the household, if:

- This is their usual or only place of residence,

OR

- A place of residence is maintained for them both here and elsewhere.

Persons absent at the time of contact should be included as members of the household if a place of residence is held for them here and if *no* place of residence is held for them elsewhere.

If none of these criteria applies, include the person in the household, but tell us what you can about the situation. (See Illustration 12-1 on page 93.)

Designation of Respondent Family Relationship

Sometimes study directors want to obtain information about families and believe that a certain person within each family will be the best source of information. In these cases, we often designate one respondent from each family living within the sample HU. This means you must first determine how many family units there are and who belongs in each one.

Family Units

A family unit consists of household members who are related to each other by blood, marriage, or adoption. A person unrelated to other occupants in the HU — or living alone — constitutes a family unit with only one member. Once you know the family units, you will be ready to determine the primary one.

• *Primary Family Unit.* If there is more than one family in the household, you will probably need to ask a question or two in order to determine which family is primary. Try to determine which family owns or rents the home. If families share ownership or rent equally, the one whose head is closest to age 45 is usually considered to be the primary family.

• *Secondary Family Unit.* A secondary family is any family (of one or more members) in the HU *unrelated to the primary family*. There may be more than one secondary family in an HU.

Family Relationships

• *Head of Family.* The most common listing situation is a married couple living alone or with their minor children. In this situation, the husband is always the head of the family according to our definition. This rule holds true even if the husband is disabled or unemployed and the wife is supporting the family.

In other situations, we consider the family head to be the "economic dominant." In order to determine who is the economic dominant, you will need to obtain some additional information about the family's financial arrangements. At this stage of interviewing, it is generally NOT a good idea to inquire about income. However, you can ask such general questions as:

> Which of these people (the ones recorded in the listing box) are working?

Choosing Respondents

Who provides the major share of financial support for the family? (Who is the main breadwinner?)

Questions like these should enable you to determine fairly accurately whom we would consider the economic dominant. For instance, if there is only one employed person, that person should be considered the head.

If it is still unclear which person is the economic dominant — and there will undoubtedly be cases in which it will be unclear — we are interested in the person who is *economically most active*. If, for example, an unemployed widow (living on a pension) has a middle-aged daughter who is actively involved in earning a living, we would consider the daughter the head of the family even though the mother owns the house.

Sometimes different members of a family have equal economic power; for example, two unmarried sisters with equal incomes may share expenses equally. In such cases, if all other things are equal, the one closest to age 45 is considered the family head.

NOTE: *In the case of a married couple, the husband is ALWAYS the head, even if the wife earns most or all of the income.*

To help you decide who is the family head, the above rules can be summarized with the following mnemonic device:

    Husband

    Economic dominant

    Age 45

    Do not expect your informant to know our definition of a family head. Determine it yourself on the basis of these criteria.

- *Head of Household.* The head of the primary family unit is the head of the household.

Listing Procedures

- *Number the family units* in the indicated column of the listing box. Number all listed members of the primary family "1;" number all members of the first listed secondary family "2;" number members of the next listed secondary family "3;" and so on (see column (d) in Illustration 12-2). Each of the persons listed in the HU must have a family unit number.

- *Make out a secondary family cover sheet* for each secondary family unit *if* the study requires that all families be included. The cover sheet originally assigned to the sample HU is for the primary family unit. Make out a *secondary family* cover sheet for each secondary family present in the HU; on secondary family cover sheets, be sure to record the address exactly as it appears on the cover sheet for the primary family in this HU.

- *Check the designated respondent* in the appropriate column of the listing box (see column (e) in Illustration 12-2). When the designated respondent is unavailable for the entire study period, some studies will instruct you to select an alternate respondent for the family. This is permissible only when the unit of interest for all or part of the study is a family rather than an individual.

Designation of the Respondent by Selection Table

When we wish to represent all adults in the U.S. or all citizens of voting age or all persons between the ages of 16 and 25, we are likely to find more than one eligible person in an HU. Since we may not wish to confine our choice to the head of the family, or to the wife of the head of

Illustration 12-2
RESPONDENT SELECTION BY FAMILY RELATIONSHIP — COVER SHEET FOR PRIMARY FAMILY

SURVEY RESEARCH CENTER
INSTITUTE FOR SOCIAL RESEARCH
THE UNIVERSITY OF MICHIGAN
ANN ARBOR, MICHIGAN 48106

(Do not write in above space.)

1. Interviewer's Label
2. Primary Area __Washtenaw__
3. Your Interview No. __10__
4. Date __May 19, 1975__
5. Length of Interview __67__ (Minutes)
6. Segment No. __1003 B__
7. Line No. __7__
8. Address (or description) __1202 Olivia Street__
9. Location __Ann Arbor__
10. State __Michigan   48104__

11. For this segment, the entry in Column 6 of the Blue Segment Folder is: (CHECK ONE)

   ☒ HEAD
   Interview Head of Family

   ☐ WIFE
   Interview Wife of Head of Family if Head is married; interview Head if Head is not married.

12. LIST ALL PERSONS, INCLUDING CHILDREN LIVING IN THE HOUSING UNIT, BY THEIR RELATIONSHIP TO THE HEAD.

(a) Household Members by Relationship to Head	(b) Sex	(c) Age	(d) Family Unit Number	(e) Enter "R" for Respondent
1. HEAD OF HOUSEHOLD	M	44	1	R
2. Wife	F	42	1	
3. Son	M	18	1	
4. Daughter	F	13	1	
5. Roomer	M	20	2	
6. Roomer	M	19	3	
7. Mother-in-law	F	65	1	
8.				

Choosing Respondents

the family, or to another specific family member, we must use a method which gives all eligible persons in the HU a chance for selection. When respondents are to be selected in this way, there will be a selection table on the cover sheet. (See Selection Table D in Illustration 12-3.)

Number Each Eligible* Person

Assign number "1" to the oldest male, number "2" to the next oldest male, and so on, until all eligible males are numbered. Continue the number sequence, numbering eligible females from oldest to youngest; the oldest female gets the next number after the youngest male, etc.

Check Selection Table

Refer to the selection table on the cover sheet and circle the number in the left hand column corresponding to the total number of eligible persons *listed* in the HU. In the right hand column of the selection table, opposite the number of eligible persons, is the number of the person to be interviewed; circle that number (Illustration 12-3).

Select Respondent

Find the person whose number you have selected and put an "R" beside his (or her) number in the "respondent" column of the listing box. *This is the selected respondent; you are to interview him (or her) and no one else.* An illustration of how a respondent is selected within a household through the use of the selection table appears in Illustration 12-4. This illustration shows a listing box from the 1972 election study.

To be *eligible* for selection, the household member must have been a U.S. citizen and at least 18 years of age before the election on November 7. Note that the interviewer had to ask about the birthday of the 17 year-old son in order to determine his eligibility in column (d). There are five eligible persons in this household. The 47 year-old head is the oldest male and is numbered "1." The 21 year-old son is the next oldest male and is numbered "2," and so on. Selection Table D used in the example indicates that if there is a total of five eligible people in the household, person number "4" (in this case the son who will be 18 before November 7) is the respondent.

Interview Only Person Selected

Interview only the person indicated by the Selection Table. If the selected person is not at home, ask about the best times to return for an interview. If the selected respondent will not be home during the survey, *do not* substitute anyone else for the original selection. If you cannot obtain an interview with the selected respondent, classify the HU as noninterview (NI - RU, or Ref., etc.; see page 99).

NONRESPONSE CLASSIFICATION

HU's which belong in the following five categories can usually be classified early in the study period. As soon as you have classified a cover sheet into one of these categories, return it to the Ann Arbor office.

Status Categories

- *SLIP — Sample Listing Isn't Proper.* The listing as it is given does not describe an HU that qualifies for sampling. This may be for one of several reasons: there may be no HU at the address; all quarters at the listed address may be excluded; the address may be outside the established survey boundaries, and so forth. Give a full description of the situation in the space provided for comments.

- *NER — No Eligible Respondent.* No one at the address is eligible to be interviewed, according to the study definition. For example, they may all be noncitizens or underage.

---

* Eligibility for each study is defined in the study instruction book.

Illustration 12-3
RESPONDENT SELECTION USING SELECTION TABLE — LISTING BOX FROM THE 1972 ELECTION STUDY

List ALL household members by relationship to Head

	(a) Household members by relationship to Head	(b) Sex	(c) Age	(d) If 17: Will he/she Be 18 on or Before Nov 7? "Yes" or "No"	(e) Citizen? "Yes" or "No"	(f) Eligible Persons " "	(g) Person Number	(h) Enter "R" for Respondent
Persons 17 years or over	HEAD OF HOUSEHOLD	M	47		Yes	✓	1	
	Wife	F	45		No			
	sister-in-law	F	30		No			
	daughter	F	23		Yes	✓	5	
	son	M	21		Yes	✓	2	
	son	M	19		Yes	✓	3	
	son	M	17	Yes	Yes	✓	4	R
Persons under 17 years	daughter	F	15					

SELECTION TABLE D

If the number of eligible persons is:	Interview the person numbered:
1	1
2	2
3	2
4	3
⑤	④
6 or more	4

For d. For 17 year olds, you must ascertain whether they will be 18 on or before November 7 and write "yes" or "no" in this column.

For e. Ask "Are any of these persons not U.S. Citizens?" (Write "no" for ones who aren't and "yes" for all others.)

For f. Enter a check mark ( ) for each person eligible for selection. Eligible persons are U.S. Citizens 18 years of age or older (and 17 year olds who will be 18 on or before November 7).

For g. Assign a sequential number to each eligible person checked in column (f). Number checked Males in household from oldest to youngest, THEN number checked Females in household from oldest to youngest.

For h. Use the selection table on the lower right of the listing box to determine the number of the person to be interviewed. In the first column of the selection table, circle the number of eligible persons. The number across from this circled number in the second column of the selection table identifies the person to be interviewed. In column (h), enter the letter R to identify that person as your respondent.

- *HV — House Vacant.* A year-round HU is not being lived in, and you obtained no indication of occupancy on calls you made during the interviewing period before you learned that the HU was vacant.

- *SV — Seasonal Vacancy.* An HU intended for occupancy only during certain seasons is not being lived in on the first call. The first call is made on a regular weekday (Monday noon to Friday noon, but not a holiday). If it appears as if no one will return at night, then consider the seasonal unit vacant for the entire study.

- *VTS — Vacant Trailer Space.* If, on your first call, a trailer *space* in a regular trailer park does not have a trailer parked on it, consider the space vacant for the entire study. Unoccupied trailers are to be classified HV, SV, or SLIP, depending on the way in which they are being used.

Summary Categories

The following classifications are summary categories to be used when efforts to obtain an interview have not been successful.

- *NOC(AT) — No Occupant Contacted at Any Time.* The HU seems to be occupied but no one was at home during any of the required number of calls. Most nonresponse forms have two NOC(AT) categories: one to use if you are able to complete the household composition box from information you obtain from reliable sources such as neighbors or building superintendents; the other to use when you are not able to determine the household composition.

NOTE: NOC must be used on the call record to record the results of a specific call when you find no one home at an occupied HU. NOC(AT) must be used only on the nonresponse form when you are unable to contact the people living at an occupied HU on any call.

- *RU — Respondent Unavailable.* Someone in the HU has been contacted, but the selected respondent is temporarily absent or unavailable, although he might be available at some future time. This covers situations in which the respondent is traveling, in the hospital, or at work when you call.

- *Ref — Refusal.* Be sure to request a persuasion letter from the Ann Arbor office if there is any hope of converting a refusal to an interview. On the nonresponse form, describe the circumstances and reasons given for refusing, and specify who refused as follows:

—*Ref(R)* The selected respondent refused to grant the interview.

—*Ref(O)* The interview was refused by someone other than the respondent.

—*Ref(U)* The refusal occurred before a household listing was obtained so that the respondent is undetermined.

- *NI — Other.* This category includes all reasons for nonresponse other than those specifically listed above. Some situations which fall into this "NI-Other" category are respondents with permanent mental or health conditions which make an interview impossible, language barriers, evasive respondents, or respondents who moved after you knew the HU to be occupied. Be sure to give a complete description of the situation.

13 OFFICE FORMS AND RECORDS

This chapter describes the procedure by which you will be paid for the work you do for the Center. This payment involves reimbursement for miles you travel by car and other expenses you incur, in addition to salary for the time you spend traveling and working for the University.

Three forms are used to report time and expenses:

- The *Time Sheet* is used to report time worked.
- The *Travel Expense Report* is used to report mileage and other expenses.
- The *Mileage Statement* is used to itemize miles traveled on each trip, and must be attached to the Travel Expense Report.

It is your responsibility to keep the required records for claiming time and expenses and to submit them regularly according to the schedule. Carefully complete, check, and double check all forms for accuracy before mailing them to the Field Office. If you make any errors, the records may be returned to you for correction, and payment will be delayed.

The following instructions apply to all three forms:

- *Copies sent to the Field Office are to be filled out in ink or typewritten.*
- *Signatures on all copies are to be written in ink.*
- *All forms are to be submitted regularly every two weeks* in accordance with the schedule provided unless you have no time or expenses to claim for a given period. Do not accumulate time and expenses and submit a claim covering several periods at one time.
- *Keep copies of all pay forms you send to the Field Office,* in case a form is lost in the mail or in case some question should arise between you and the Field Office. The University cannot provide copies of the pay forms for tax purposes at the end of the year.

To ensure prompt delivery of your pay records, send them in the postage paid, preaddressed envelopes we provide. Do *not* add the name of any other University department on the front of your envelope. Do *not* include pay records with any interviews or sampling materials which you may be sending to the Field Office.

TIME SHEET

Your pay for the hours you work for the University is based on the information you record on the Time Sheets. You must complete these forms carefully and in accordance with the instructions printed on the back in order to receive payment for all of the hours you work. After the pay checks are written, the Time Sheets are microfilmed and kept on permanent file by the University.

As a University of Michigan hourly employee, you will be paid every two weeks. Each pay period begins on Sunday and ends on Saturday two weeks later. A schedule of the specific starting and ending dates for each of the bi-weekly pay periods in an entire year will be sent to you before the beginning of each fiscal year on July 1. You must submit your Time Sheets in accordance with this schedule; that is, each Time Sheet must show one of the Sunday starting dates indicated on the Bi-Weekly Pay Schedule, and must include only time worked between that date and the indicated Saturday ending date (Illustration 13-1). The month, day, and year of the starting date is to be written on the line of the Time Sheet under the heading "FIRST DAY OF REPORTING PERIOD." This date must be recorded in that space even if you did not work on that day — or even if you did not work at all during the first week of the given reporting period.

The schedule card also shows the date by which Time Sheets must be received here in the Field Office in order to be processed for payment and still allow sufficient time for checks to be written and mailed from the University Payroll Office on the "Pay Date" for each period on the schedule card. Since there are only four days between the end of a pay period and the due date, you must send your completed Time Sheet in immediately after the last day of the pay period so that it can be included with the current payroll. If a Time Sheet arrives late, it must be held over and processed for the next pay date. Late time will be combined with any time you submit for the next period and one check covering the combined amount will be sent.

The project accounts are kept open for a reasonable period after the close of interviewing to allow us to pay interviewers whose Time Sheets have been delayed either in the mail or because of processing problems. Once the project account has been closed, no further time or expense charges against that project will be accepted.

Be prepared to work at least 20 hours a week when a study is in the field. If you are working on more than one study at a time, you may need to work more than the usual number of hours. Please note, however, *that you are not authorized to work more than 40 hours in one week.* In unusual circumstances, the Field Office may give you permission to work more than 40 hours, and they will send instructions for completing a special Time Sheet.

A hypothetical Time Sheet has been filled out (Illustration 13-1). Note that the only *date* appearing on the Time Sheet is the "FIRST DAY OF REPORTING PERIOD" Sunday, February 16, 1975. Without this date, the actual dates the interviewer worked could not be determined and the Time Sheet would have to be returned for clarification. Please be sure to place your name label on the top left-hand corner of the Time Sheet as noted. The designation "TEMPORARY HOURLY . . . " in the box at the top of the Time Sheet is a classification used by the University for part-time employees and does not refer to the length of the appointment.

MILEAGE STATEMENT

Interviewers usually use their own cars while they are working. You will be reimbursed for the use of your car on a per mile basis. You should also report toll charges and, in some cases, parking. The Mileage Statement, which has step-by-step instructions printed on the back, is the form on which mileage claims are to be submitted. Illustration 13-2 is a completed Mileage Statement.

In filling out a Mileage Statement, keep in mind the following general instructions:

• Submit one copy for payment, along with the required two copies of the related Travel Expense Report (discussed later in this chapter) on which mileage costs are claimed.

• The Mileage Statement submitted in any given pay period should cover all mileage claimed during that period.

• Do *not* use tenth-of-a-mile readings from your odometer; ENTER THE ENTIRE READING (rounded to the nearest *full* mile), not just the last three digits.

• Odometer readings must not overlap on a single Mileage Statement or from one Mileage Statement to the next. If you use more than one car during the course of your work, be sure to note this on the Mileage Statement in case a question arises about the difference in odometer entries. A simple explanation at the bottom of the form is sufficient.

• Do not use resettable trip-meter readings.

TRAVEL EXPENSE REPORT (TER)

The Travel Expense Report is the official form for claiming payment for mileage and other allowable out-of-pocket expenses which you incur while working for the University. A copy of every travel report submitted is kept in the University's permanent files. If there are errors, incomplete details, or items that cannot be accepted for payment, the form must be returned to you for correction, and payment will be delayed. *Double check the Travel Expense Report for accuracy before sending it to the Field Office.*

Although we ask that you submit the Travel Expense Report with the Time Sheet, the expense forms follow a different path through University accounting procedures. First they are checked for errors, approved for payment, then keypunched for input to the computer which writes the checks on the 10th and last *working* days of each month. Your expense check is separate from your payroll check, which is written every two weeks. In general, you should expect to receive your expense check about two weeks later than your payroll check for the same pay period.

In completing Travel Expense Reports, you should follow these general instructions:

• Submit Travel Expense Reports (including the separate Mileage Statement) at the end of each pay period, except when you are on special assignment outside of your primary area or if expenses for that pay period amount to less than $5.00.

If expenses for a pay period amount to less than $5.00, please wait to submit them until the following pay period. Processing small claims is very expensive and the University will not write checks for less than $1.00.

• If you are traveling on special assignment outside your primary area and are to be away overnight, you will receive special instructions and a special form for keeping track of your expenses. Travel Expense Reports for trips away from home may be sent to Ann Arbor immediately after the trip is completed.

• Travel Expense Reports come in sets of three. *Submit only the white and yellow copies* to the Field Office with your Mileage Statement when claiming expenses; the blue copy is for your personal file. Disregard the note printed on the top of the form which instructs you to "submit in triplicate . . ."

• The white copy must be *an original on both sides.* It goes into the University's permanent files; the yellow copy is kept on file in the Center's Business Office and may be a carbon copy, if it is legible — *except for the signature, which must be in ink.*

• You must obtain a receipt for any expense of $1.00 or more and attach it to the expense report for reimbursement. Occasionally, you may make several payments for the same purpose at different times during a day; for example, a

Illustration 13-1
TIME SHEET

SOC. SEC. 003-13-1717
NAME — ADAIR, ALLISON
5 SOUTHFIELD CIRCLE
WESTPORT, MICHIGAN
48103

(FIELD STAFF PLACE LABEL ABOVE)

TOTAL HOURS: 40.4

FIRST DAY OF REPORTING PERIOD:
SUNDAY, Feb. (MONTH) 16 (DATE) 1975 (YEAR)

REPORT TIME TO NEAREST TENTH OF AN HOUR, SEE REVERSE SIDE.

DAY	TOTAL DAILY HOURS	455691	457751	495325	457680	
SUN						
MON	4.5	2.5	2.0			
TUE	1.2	1.2				
WED	2.0	2.0				
THUR	6.7			3.7	3.0	
FRI	2.7				2.7	
SAT						
WEEK'S TOTAL	17.1					
SUN	3.0		3.0			
MON						
TUE	4.5		4.5			
WED		5.4	4.4			
THUR						
FRI	6.0	3.0		3.0		
SAT						
WEEK'S TOTAL	23.3					
TOTAL HOURS BY PROJECT		14.1	13.9	6.7	5.7	

I certify I have worked the hours shown above.

Allison Adair (SIGNATURE)

TITLE: Interviewer

TEMPORARY HOURLY TIME SHEET
INSTITUTE FOR SOCIAL RESEARCH

RATE: _____

BUSINESS OFFICE USE ONLY

TEMP. HRLY. ___ 02 ___
P/R DATE ___

TOTAL PAY ___

PAY PERIOD CODE ___

PROJECT NO.   HOURS   CLASS

02 ___
03 ___
04 ___

APPROVAL ___
DATE ___ REF. NO. ___

Illustration 13-1 (continued)

INSTRUCTIONS: FILL OUT LEFT SIDE ONLY

AT BEGINNING OF REPORTING PERIOD:

1. Print name and social security number at top of sheet in ink. (Field Staff place label).
2. Enter date on which the reporting period starts in proper space.

ON EACH DAY YOU WORK:

3. Enter all time to the nearest tenth of an hour (see table below). Record whole hours in the wide space to the left of the dotted line, and tenths in the smaller space to the right.
4. Enter hours worked that day under left hand column headed total daily hours.
5. Show breakdown of total daily hours per project by using one column for each project, entering the project number at the top and the hours worked underneath it opposite the day worked. Use an additional time sheet if you work on more than five projects during a reporting period.

BEFORE SUBMITTING YOUR TIME SHEET:

6. Add daily total and hours by project.
7. Sign your name in ink.
8. Time sheet must have signature of approval. (Field Interviewers' time will be approved in Field Office).

9. TABLE

Minutes	Tenths of hour
1 - 2	0 - round down to hour
3 - 8	1
9 - 14	2
15 - 20	3
21 - 26	4
27 - 32	5
33 - 38	6
39 - 44	7
45 - 50	8
51 - 56	9
57 - 60	0 - round up to hour

10. EXAMPLE

DAY	TOTAL DAILY HOURS	PROJECT NUMBER(S)				
		459750	480246	457680		
SUN						
MON	8.0	6.1	1.9			
TUE	7.5		3.5	4.0		

Illustration 13-2
MILEAGE STATEMENT

Field Office, Survey Research Center   MILEAGE STATEMENT (Complete in INK!)   The University of Michigan

DATE	ITINERARY FROM	TO	SPEEDOMETER READINGS START	SPEEDOMETER READINGS END	MILES	PERSONAL USE	MILES PER PROJECT Proj.# 45591	Proj.# 457151	Proj.# 457680
2/17	Home to Mercy Hospital	home	42700	42736	36		36		
2/17	Home to Segment 2001B, 2003A	home	42743	42767	24			24	
2/18	Home to Mercy Hospital	home	42781	42817	36		36		
2/19	" " " "	"	42825	42868	43	7	36		
2/20	Home to chunk 1112	home	42873	42898	25				25
2/21	Dauphie's house to chunk 3032	home	42903	42918	15				15
2/23	Home to segments 1173D, 1175C, 1124B	home	42926	42938	12			12	
2/25	Home to segment 1124B	home	42945	42955	10	2		8	
2/26	Home to Mercy Hospital, seg. 1173D, 1175C	home	42960	43005	45		18	27	
2/28	Home to Mercy Hospital	home	43018	43054	36		36		
						A. TOTAL MILES BY PROJECT	162	71	40
						B. ALLOWANCE PER MILE	14	14	14
						C. EXPENSES CLAIMED BY PROJECT (A×B)	22.68	9.94	5.60

003-13-1717 ADAIR, ALLISON
5 SOUTHFIELD CIRCLE
WESTPORT, MICHIGAN
48103

Allison Adair
SIGNATURE

I certify that this statement is correct, that the amount charged for mileage was reasonable, necessary, and in discharge of official business; and that the above account or any part of it has not heretofore been allowed or paid.

Illustration 13-2 (continued)

Step-by-step procedures for completing the Mileage Statement

1. Interviewer's Label: Your name label goes in the space provided at the bottom of the form.

2. Date: Enter the numerals for the month and date of each day you traveled for the Center.

3. Itinerary From and To: Under "From" list your starting point. For example, "home." If you begin one of your trips from somewhere other than your home, identify the starting place by the address or nearest intersection. Under "to" list your destinations in the order in which you visit them. The last mentioned destination is to be the point at which you finish travel for the Center. A typical listing might be "Segments 203A, 106B, 122F and home."

4. Speedometer Readings: The columns should show the complete readings on your speedometer, rounded to the nearest full mile, at the start of the trip (the starting point listed under "From") and the reading at the end of the trip (the last listed place under "To"). If more than one car is used, make a note to this effect on the bottom of the form.

5. Miles: The number of miles is simply the speedometer reading at the end of your trip minus the reading at the start of your trip.

6. Personal Use: Enter miles traveled during the course of a recorded trip which were not on official University business. For example, if you have traveled two miles out of the most direct route between segments to pick up dry cleaning, enter "2" in this column - opposite the appropriate date and trip. This amount can then be easily subtracted before allotting the miles by project.

7. Miles Per Project: The miles traveled on each trip must be allotted by project. Do this by entering the project number(s) at the top of the column, and underneath it, on the appropriate line, enter the miles chargeable to that project. Whenever you work on more than one project in the course of a single trip, you are expected to divide the miles as accurately as possible among all the projects you worked on.

8. Total Miles By Project: At the end of the pay period, add up the miles claimed on each project.

9. Allowance By Mile: Enter the current mileage allowance.

10. Expenses Claimed By Project: Multiply the total miles by the allowance per mile. THE RESULTING DOLLAR FIGURES (BY PROJECT) ARE THOSE WHICH YOU WILL TRANSFER TO THE BACK OF THE TRAVEL EXPENSE REPORT.

11. Signature: Sign the completed form in ink.

Illustration 13-3
TRAVEL EXPENSE REPORT

TRAVEL EXPENSE REPORT

THE UNIVERSITY OF MICHIGAN, ANN ARBOR, MICHIGAN

Bank Code (7-8)—51

~~(Submit in Triplicate to the TRAVEL OFFICE)~~

Name of Traveler (9-23) _____ Last _____ First _____ Middle

~~Departure ___ Date ___ Time~~

~~Return ___ Date ___ Time~~

~~Destination~~ (24-38)

```
003-13-1717   ADAIR, ALLISON
              5 SOUTHFIELD CIRCLE
              WESTPORT, MICHIGAN
              48103
```

	Account Number (39-44)	Amount (45-53)	Trip Number (57-62)	Class Code (63-66)
Expenses Claimed				2800
				2800
				2800
				2800
				2800
Less Advances From: Cashier	990070	( )		0000
Leave Blank		( )		
		( )		
Leave Blank		( )		

DO NOT WRITE IN THIS SPACE. IT IS FOR BUSINESS OFFICE USE ONLY.

Purpose of Trip:

Travel + expenses incurred on Projects 455691, 457751 and 457680

I hereby certify that this claim is correct, is reimbursable under published travel regulations of the University of Michigan, and reimbursement has not, and will not, be obtained from any other source:

Feb 28, 1975   **Allison Adair**
Date   Signature of Traveler

_____ Date   _____ Signature of Person Authorizing the Travel (A)

_____ Date   _____ Signature of Authorized Signer for the Account

~~The three signature lines cannot authorize and ap~~ | ~~signatures are required, as the traveler~~
~~Submit in Triplicate to the~~ | ~~spital and direct any questions to:~~
~~Travel Office—North~~
~~University Hospital~~
~~Institute for Social Research, 1106 ISR Building, 764-8354~~

INTERVIEWERS SHOULD DISREGARD THE ITEMS WHICH ARE CROSSED OUT ON THIS FORM

PASSED BY ACCOUNTING DEPARTMENT

Note: White Copy Accounting Department, Yellow Copy Accounting Department, ~~Blue Copy Travel Office~~

(1-6) Voucher No. (71-76)

Form 6900 Revised 5/75

Illustration 13-3 (continued)

ITEMIZED TRAVEL EXPENSES

REFER TO TRAVEL PROCEDURE (#204.1) FOR SPECIFIC INSTRUCTIONS. UNIVERSITY HOSPITAL EMPLOYEES SHOULD ALSO REFER TO THE HOSPITAL STANDARD PRACTICE GUIDE (#199).

Date	Description (State Purchase Order Number When Applicable)	Amount Claimed
	Prepaid Airfare (PO #) — Amount:	
	Prepaid Registration Fees (PO #) — Amount:	
2/20	Mailed interview + cassette to supervisor (receipt attached) P.455691	1.75
2/17-2/28	Mileage claimed (statement attached)	
	162 miles @ .14 per mile P.455691	22.68
	71 miles @ .14 per mile P.457751	9.94
	40 miles @ .14 per mile P.457680	5.60
2/17-2/28	4 parking charges @ 1.00 Mercy Hospital lot (receipt attached) P.455691	4.00
2/28	6 phone calls from booth at Mercy Hospital @ .10 — appointments for P.455691	.60
1/17-2/15	Telephone calls plus 12% Tax (receipt attached)	
	P.457751	1.49
	P.457680	4.07
2/25	Interpreter's fee (receipt attached) 1 interview @ 20.00	20.00

Itemize the following by date:	Date	Date	Date	Date	Date	Date	Date
Lodging							
Meals*: Breakfast		THIS SECTION OF THE EXPENSE REPORT IS TO BE USED ONLY WHEN YOU ARE ON SPECIAL ASSIGNMENT AWAY FROM YOUR PRIMARY AREA.					
Lunch							
Dinner							

* Including Tip

TOTAL **70.13**

Instructions:

1) All reimbursable expenses must be listed and appropriate receipts attached. Expenses paid for in advance, through Purchasing, must be listed with the Purchase Order # referenced. (Do not list such paid expenses in the Amount Claimed column, but attach supporting P.O. documents.)
2) University employees make checks payable to "The University of Michigan." University Hospital employees make checks payable to the "University Hospital."
3) The Traveler must sign on the reverse side in the space provided.
4) Submit Travel Expense Report within 10 days after returning from trip.

number of toll calls, bridge or highway tolls, or parking charges in which the total amount expended is more than a dollar. You will not need a receipt if you enter the rate of the expense for each item and if the *average* charge is less than $1.00. For example, "parking at Imperial Hotel and lot in Segment 8001B: 2 @ 75¢ — $1.50" is acceptable without a receipt, but an entry of "parking at Imperial Hotel and lot in Segment 8001B — $1.50" would require a receipt because the charge is more than $1.00.

Front of the Travel Expense Report (Illustration 13-3): Complete only the following items; leave the others blank.

1. Name of Traveler and Home Address: Place your name label in the space shown on the example on both the white and yellow copies. Your check will be made out to the name which appears on the label, and sent to the address on the label.

2. Purpose of Trip: The following simple statement is all that is necessary: "Travel and expenses incurred on Project(s) . . ." List numbers of all projects involved; for example, "Travel and expenses incurred on Projects 457680 and 455691."

3. Date and Signature of Traveler: Enter the date submitted and *sign your name in ink on both the white and yellow copies* on the lines below "Purpose of Trip" which are headed "Date" and "Signature of Traveler." Remember, unsigned reports, reports which have signatures in carbon or pencil, typewritten names, or name labels pasted on this line cannot be accepted and will be returned to you for correction. Leave all other spaces on the front of the report blank.

Back of the Travel Expense Report (Illustration 13-3): This is the "Itemized Travel Expenses" side of the form; disregard reference to "Travel Manual" and "Travel Office."

1. Date: In this column, enter the month and inclusive dates on which expenses were incurred.

2. Description: Describe the expenses you are claiming. *Put only one expense item on each line*. If you worked on *one* project during the reporting period, the project number is already entered on the front of the form and need not be entered again on the back. *If you worked on more than one project* during the reporting period, each expense item listed on the back must be assigned the number of the project to which it should be charged. Project numbers can be entered at the end of

the line on which you describe the expenditure. Miles (from the Mileage Statement) must be shown as an item of expense on the Travel Expense Report, but you only need to enter the information from items A, B, and C at the bottom of the Mileage Statement. One entry should be made for each project. (See illustration.)

Allowable expenses. The following is a basic guide to the kinds of expenses which you may claim. If you are in doubt as to whether or not an expense is allowable, or in doubt as to the proper way to enter a claim on your expense report, write to your supervisor or to the Field Office for clarification before you submit the claim.

• *Mileage:* Mileage incurred while working for the Center is an allowable expense. Include the Mileage Statement (described above) with the Travel Expense Report when claiming mileage.

• *Travel by mass transportation:* Fares for bus, subway, and other forms of mass transportation used on official business are allowable expenses. In showing more than one trip on a single day, you can lump these fares together, but be sure to show the amount of the single fare. For example, "4 bus fares at 35¢ per fare — $1.40."

• *Tolls:* Tolls or road fees on bridges, expressways, tunnels, etc., are acceptable and should be shown on the report as follows: "2 tolls on Ohio Turnpike, Exit 5 to Exit 4 and return at 80¢ each — $1.60."

• *Parking:* Whenever possible, please use free parking. In congested areas where free parking is not available, the University will pay for parking. To obtain reimbursement for parking, enter meter fees or parking lot charges on your Travel Expense Report and attach a receipt if the charge was for $1.00 or more.

• *Supplies:* You may order supplies necessary for your work from the Field Office using the *Supply Request Form;* this includes all materials from study forms to writing pads and pencils. Try to allow sufficient time for the supplies to reach you before you run out. On occasions when we cannot supply you with essential items, you may make small purchases and enter the item on your Travel Expense Report; attach a receipt if the item costs $1.00 or more. Consult the Field Office before making supply or equipment purchases of $5.00 or more.

• *Postage:* You may order prepaid envelopes, both letter size and large manila ones, for mailing to the Field Office. Postage charges for materials sent to your supervisor or supplies sent to other interviewers are also allowable expenses. When entering postage charges on your Travel

Expense Report, show to whom you were mailing materials and attach a receipt if the charge was $1.00 or more (Illustration 13-3).

• *Interpreters:* You may encounter a respondent whose English is too poor to permit an interview. On most studies, we would like you to see if another household member or a neighbor could serve as interpreter for you. If it seems appropriate, you may pay this nonprofessional interpreter up to $5.00; obtain a signed receipt and submit the expense for reimbursement on your Travel Expense Report (Illustration 13-3).

If no suitable interpreter can be found in the household or neighborhood, identify the language the potential respondent speaks and then see if you will have three or more respondents on the study who must be interviewed in that language. If there are only one or two, return the cover sheets as "noninterview — language." If you have three or more such respondents, attempt to locate a skilled translator to accompany you and translate the questions and the respondents' answers while you record the information in the questionnaire. Pay the translator at the flat rate of $25.00 per interview. Be sure to obtain a signed receipt and submit it with your Travel Expense Report. We do not pay mileage or other expenses for interpreters.

If you run into a situation not covered by these instructions, consult the Field Office.

• *Escorts:* On some special occasions your supervisor may authorize the use of a driver or escort. Pay the driver/escort at the rate of a beginning interviewer in your primary area. You must obtain a signed receipt from the driver/escort showing the number of hours worked and the rate at which he/she was paid.

When you request your supervisor's permission to use an escort, let her know the areas you will be working in and the approximate length of time the escort will be needed. Your supervisor will send you permission in writing with a copy to the Field Office.

• *Telephone calls:* All telephone calls to the Field Office in Ann Arbor should be collect, station-to-station calls. You should also call your supervisor collect as she can charge the call to the University by using her credit card. You may, however, have to place some calls from public telephones while you are working, and you may also have charges for telephone calls to respondents on telephone studies. The total amount for local telephone calls made from a pay station should be shown separately on your expense report, as indicated in Illustration 13-3.

Claims on all long distance calls from your home must be accompanied by your telephone bill (or a photocopy of it). The total amount of these calls on *each* project, plus the federal, state, and local tax (if any) charged on that amount, should be entered on one line of the Travel Expense Report as shown below.

Note the tax rate you use to figure the tax. For 1975 the federal tax on all calls is 7 percent; it is scheduled to be reduced by 1 percent each year, so that in 1976, it will be 6 percent; in 1977, 5 percent, etc. Check with your local phone company for state and local tax rates.

Be sure to put a project number on the telephone bill next to each call for which you are claiming reimbursement. Cross out those calls which are *not* being charged to University projects. (See example.) When possible, figure the tax directly on the phone bill.

A special form, the *Telephone Call Record,* should be used if you are claiming *unit* calls that are not listed individually on your telephone bill. This form can be obtained from the Field Office by checking the appropriate box on the Supply Request Form. Please be sure to read and follow carefully the instructions on the back of the Telephone Call Record before you submit it.

Claims that are not allowed. A few items cannot be accepted as legitimate expense claims. Please familiarize yourself with these items so that you will not incur unnecessary costs to yourself.

• *Car insurance:* Part of the mileage allowance is intended to cover insurance and road service as well as gasoline and oil. It is your responsibility to carry your own car insurance. This includes coverage for any damages due to an accident, fire, theft, towing fees, etc.

• *Traffic or parking tickets:* The University cannot reimburse you for any traffic violations or parking tickets regardless of when such fines are incurred.

• *Meals:* Claims for meals are usually *not* allowable, just as they are not if you work in an office. But if you are asked by the office or supervisor to travel away from your primary area on a special assignment for eight hours or more (not overnight), you may claim meals which you had to buy because of the length of time you spent away from home. Usually this means you may claim lunch, and sometimes you might have to buy breakfast or dinner. The maximum amount you can claim for each meal is $2.25 for breakfast, $3.50 for lunch, and $8.50 for dinner. You do not need a receipt to claim expenses for a meal, but you must have obtained permission from your supervisor before the trip.

• *Taxi fares:* Taxi fares are generally not allowable in a primary area where it is possible to use your personal car or mass transportation. However, taxi fares are allowable expenses if you are working on assignment away from your primary area and it is more expedient to use a taxi than other means of transportation, for example, from the airport to the hotel. It is not necessary to obtain a receipt for these expenses.

PAYROLL PRACTICES

Pay rates and raises. The Survey Research Center gives two types of pay raises:

• *General rate change raises* granted periodically to all our interviewers "across the board . . ."

• *Raises (promotions) given for merit* after an interviewer has completed a certain number of interviews for which "*experience points*" are given, and submitted a taped interview to the supervisor for evaluation.

Consideration for advancement to the next level is given upon completion of the probationary period, and then again upon accumulation of 150, 300, 450, 600, and each additional 300 experience points.

You will also be evaluated by your supervisor either through personal observation or through a tape recorded interview which will then be "observed" by your supervisor using a coding technique. Your work will be evaluated by the Field Office at this time.

The number of points being given is shown in the instruction book for each study. Points are posted at the end of each study.

Notice of promotions, pay increases, and the effective dates will be sent to you as soon as they are approved. Pay increases *are not* retroactive.

The training allowance is indicated on the current pay schedule. The basic rate goes into effect as soon as training is finished, and is slightly higher in metropolitan areas. The supervisor will let you know the rate for your primary area.

Field Coordinators for each study receive extra points to reimburse them for the clerical work they do in keeping track of the sample and for submitting progress reports: one point for each seven days a study is in the field or for each progress and completion report, whichever is greater; also 1/2 point for each segment assigned to their primary area and/or 1/8 point per name on a name sample.

Deductions from your paycheck. Deductions for income tax and Social Security are subtracted from your pay. A withholding statement (W-2 form) indicating total annual wages and the total amounts of income tax and Social Security deductions is sent to University employees from the University Payroll Office at the end of each calendar year. If you have not received your record of earnings and deductions by February 1, notify the Field Office so that we can trace it.

A Social Security number is required of all Center employees; this number must appear on the W-4 form (Withholding Exemption Certificate), one of the forms you must complete at the time of hiring. Michigan has a state income tax and deductions are made from all wages paid by Michigan employers unless the special "exclusion certificate" is completed and signed by out-of-state employees. Your "state of employment" is the state in which you reside.

Insurance coverage. All employees of the Center are covered under Workmen's Compensation and Employer's Liability Insurance provided by the University at no expense to its employees. In general, coverage is provided for injuries sustained by interviewers while they are pursuing Center business. If an injury does occur while you are working for the Center, you will be compensated for loss of time and cost for medical services. In the event of such an injury, notify the Field Office immediately and tell us what happened. The necessary forms will be sent to you with instructions on how to complete them.

As was mentioned previously, automobile insurance is carried only on cars owned by the University. You are responsible for providing your own car insurance.

14 ADMINISTRATIVE PROCEDURES

COMMUNICATION

The first things you need to know about communication are some essential addresses and telephone numbers:

The Field Office: (U.S. Mail)
: Field Office
Survey Research Center
The University of Michigan
P.O. Box 1248
Ann Arbor, Michigan 48106

The Field Office: (Street Address)
: If you come to visit us or send a package by United Parcel Service (UPS) you will need our street address:
Field Office
Institute for Social Research
426 Thompson
Ann Arbor, Michigan 48108

Telephone: Area Code 313, 764-8356

Your supervisor:

Name: _____

Address: _____

City, State: _____

Telephone: _____ / _____
            Area Code   Number

Correspondence. Writing is our standard mode of communication. Each interviewer receives a supply of white, bright pink, and bright yellow correspondence forms to use in writing the office and the supervisor, plus a supply of preaddressed, postage paid envelopes. The white form is for regular memos; the bright pink form ("Immediate Action") and the bright yellow form ("Immediate Action — Sampling") are easily seen in a pile of correspondence, and memos written on these forms receive attention first.

Please use the standard white, pink, and yellow forms when writing to the Field Office. Little slips of paper and odd-sized letters are hard to file and easy to lose!

Always put your full name, your primary area, and the date on all correspondence. Do not assume that we will know who sent it because your name is on the envelope; the mail is sorted by project number and the envelopes are thrown away before anyone reads a memo for content.

Whatever you do, do not use the thumbnail sketch on an interview, the nonresponse form on a cover sheet, or the margins of your pay forms to ask a question, request some kind of action, or pose a problem. Memos written in these places are likely to be overlooked because interviews, cover sheets, and pay records are often sent to other sections of the Institute to be processed.

Unless a memo concerns a specific interview, do not mail it with the interviews in the large manila envelopes; instead, send correspondence separately in letter-sized envelopes. Pay forms should *never* be included in the manila envelopes with the interviews. Different people handle these two types of mail in the office, and occasionally interviews are routed to another office to be opened later. This can result in a serious delay in action on your correspondence or your pay.

The Field Office receives and sends a voluminous amount of mail, and when studies are going full swing, we receive many letters each day. Some of the problems or questions raised by interviewers require a bit of research, and the office staff must talk with people in various departments at the Center to obtain information for you. Both the volume and the nature of the correspondence contribute to the time it takes to prepare replies. Please take this into account when you write and when you are waiting for an answer. Be patient; we try not to overlook any correspondence; the office staff and supervisors realize that you thought it important or you would not have taken the time to write.

Telephone calls. There will be times when a telephone call to the office or to your supervisor will be necessary. Please place all calls to the Field Office or to your supervisor *collect*. When you are calling the Field Office, call collect, station-to-station (i.e., if the operator asks, tell her you will speak to anyone; otherwise we will be charged for a person-to-person call). Call only during office hours: 8 a.m. to 5 p.m. (Eastern Time), Monday through Friday. If the administrative assistant you need to talk to is not in the office at the time of your call, leave a brief message with the person who accepted the charge and she will see that your call is returned as soon as possible. In all cases, once you have reached the Field Office, give whomever accepts the charge the following information:

- Your full name.
- The *city and state* (*not* the primary area) from which you are calling.
- The project number of the study about which you are calling.

If you happen to be calling about scouting or sampling work which is not specifically related to a current project, give your name, city, and state to the person who accepts the charge and say you are calling about "sampling" instead of giving the project number. She will ask you for the chunk and/or segment number about which you are calling and will then find someone from the Sampling Section to talk with you. NEVER call the Sampling Section directly; make *all* contacts with study staff, sampling, or coding through the Field Office.

Whether to contact supervisor or Field Office. In some cases it may not be immediately obvious whether you should contact your supervisor or the Field Office in order to get the information you need. The following guidelines may help you decide which would be most appropriate.

Contact your *supervisor* when:

• You are faced with a personal problem that will interfere with your work or with the completion of an assignment.

• You have questions about interviewing techniques (e.g., "How should I handle a situation in which a respondent does this or that?").

• You have a question about general sampling *procedures;* (for specific sampling *problems,* contact the Field Office).

Contact the *Field Office* when:

• You must have a prompt decision from a study director or someone in the Sampling Section about which person to interview in an unusual household or whether to interview at all the HU's at an address, or to check to be sure that you have the correct address before interviewing.

• Either sampling or study materials have not arrived as expected.

• You are answering a specific request from the Field Office to *call* with some information.

• You are having difficulty somewhere in the field and need office help or even verification of your identity or interviewer status.

• You have an emergency situation that cannot be handled by written communication because of lack of time or the nature of the problem.

• You are unable to reach your supervisor.

Both the Field Office and your supervisor are there to help you. Please contact either one whenever you have a problem or need help. If you ask a question, it does not reflect poorly on your ability; on the contrary, it is intelligent to seek help when you need it.

Just as there are times when you should telephone, there are also definite times when you should *not* telephone; for example:

• *Do not call about a problem with your paycheck;* write instead, giving full details. Answers can never be obtained during a single telephone call because the problem must be traced through the business departments of the Center and the University. Moreover, checks are written by computer on a fixed schedule, so a telephone call will not speed action.

• *Do not call about future work and future assignments;* please write us about any questions you may have about this and we will reply as soon as possible.

SUPERVISORS AND FIELD COORDINATORS

The supervisor. About 15 regional supervisors share responsibility for overseeing all the Center's field interviewing. Each supervisor is responsible for hiring, training, and maintaining a staff of interviewers in the primary areas assigned to her. In the course of these duties the supervisor is in constant communication with the interviewers in each primary area through personal visits, mail, and telephone contacts.

It is the supervisor's task to evaluate each interviewer's work through tape recorded interviews and personal observation. This responsibility is discussed in greater detail in the section on evaluation, pages 120-126.

You should keep your supervisor informed about all phases of your work; let her know when you will be on vacation or out of town and therefore unavailable for assignments; let her know about any problems and difficulties you may be having as well as about the aspects of your work which you like and enjoy. She will be seeing the study directors and staff in Ann Arbor and she can relay favorable remarks or press for changes that might make your work easier.

The field coordinator. The primary areas vary considerably in physical size, sample sizes on individual studies, and interviewing conditions. Depending upon the local situation, the interviewers in any one primary area may number from 1 to 15. In a primary area staffed by only one interviewer, this person is automatically the Field Coordinator (FC). In primary areas with two or more interviewers, the supervisor may appoint one as the FC or may rotate the job, depending upon the study and interviewer availability.

An FC is the administrative contact between the primary area and the Field Office, and between the primary area and the supervisor.

The FC:

• Maintains the primary area files of materials and sampling records (maps and Yellow Folders).

- Schedules the prestudy conference.
- Holds the prestudy conference.
- Receives and distributes study materials.
- Plans with the supervisor for coverage of the sample so that work is completed within the study dates.
- Accounts for *all* sample addresses for the *weekly* progress report to supervisors and the final project completion report to supervisors and the Field Office.
- Sends the green Sample Address Summary Forms to the supervisor at the end of each study.
- Takes press releases to local newspapers and contacts local authorities.

STUDY PROCEDURES

The procedures to be followed during the course of a study are presented here in the order in which they most often occur. Although some of these steps are the responsibility of the FC, all interviewers should be familiar with them.

Primary area files. The FC keeps the primary area files which contain the Yellow Folders for the primary area's sample chunks, the Field Maps, and some general supplies. The sampling materials which you use during a study should be returned to the FC when the study is completed. Supervisors will be notified when sampling materials become obsolete and should be returned to the Field Office.

Availability forms. About six weeks before the start of interviewing, an availability memo describing the project and a standard reporting form is sent to each supervisor. The supervisor then gets in touch with the FC in each primary area to convey information about the study — dates, sample size, type of study, etc., and finds out which interviewers will be available to work during that time period. Copies of the memo are then sent to these interviewers. Mailing instructions and any anticipated problems should be noted on the availability form which is sent by the supervisor to the Field Office. Availability memos and forms are usually sent out about six weeks before the start of interviewing.

Study materials. Study materials are sent from Ann Arbor approximately 10 days before a study is scheduled to start in the field. A packet containing all materials necessary to study and complete a practice interview is mailed First Class to each interviewer working on a study. This is done to allow the interviewers time to prepare for the study before the starting date. The bulk materials, questionnaires, cover sheets, show cards, etc., are sent to the FC at the same time as the First Class packets, but by a less expensive and usually slower carrier (United Parcel Service or Fourth Class, Special Handling). Distribution of the bulk materials and sample assignments should take place at the prestudy conference if at all possible.

Prestudy conferences. In primary areas where there is more than one interviewer, all interviewers working on a study *must* attend the prestudy conference BEFORE THEY BEGIN PRODUCTION INTERVIEWING. This conference is held by the FC at a time when all the interviewers can attend. The meeting should be used to go over the practice interviews and worksheets, the question-by-question instructions, and the sampling instructions. We expect you to be completely prepared at the time of the conference and to have done the following:

- Studied all materials carefully, making notes in the instruction book of any possible problems or things you would like to discuss with the other interviewers.
- Completed the worksheet.
- Taken a practice interview and edited it.

All of the points listed below should be covered at the prestudy conference:

- *Discuss the sampling procedures thoroughly,* giving special attention to new listing, updating, and selection procedures.
- *Go over the Field Notes.* You should discuss standard field procedures as well as special instructions which appear at the beginning of the Instruction Book.
- *Go over the worksheets* together and send them to the Field Office *after* the conference. When they have been logged in, the administrative assistant in charge of the project for the Field Office will go over them, make any corrections, and return them to you.
- *Go through the practice interview* page by page, question by question, in sequence. As you review, refer to the question-by-question instructions to make sure an appropriate answer has been obtained for every question. Are the answers clear and complete? Do they meet the question objectives? Are they legible and annotated? Do you need to remind yourself to probe at a particular place? Is the thumbnail sketch informative?
- FC's should use their copy of the prestudy conference report form to keep a running

tally of each problem and proposed solution, referring to specific question numbers.

• Call the Field Office during regular business hours if there are important unresolved questions or if you anticipate difficulties and need additional information about question objectives or skip instructions.

• When the conference is over the interviewers should send their practice interviews to the supervisor and the worksheets to the Field Office. The FC should complete the prestudy conference report form and send one copy to the Field Office, one to the supervisor, and keep one in the primary area files.

Reports from these conferences help us catch problems in both the questionnaire and the procedures early in the interviewing period.

Contacting local authorities. We feel it is very important that the FC contact the local Police Chief or Sheriff (by letter or by telephone), as well as the Better Business Bureau and Chamber of Commerce and give these people the following information before interviewing begins:

• A brief statement about the study (similar to the one for respondents).

• The names of all of the local interviewers working on the study.

• A general indication of the interviewing dates and the neighborhoods where interviews will be taken.

Suggest that the above information be filed under "The University of Michigan." ISR is often confused with IRS, and there are several Survey Research Centers.

If you are interviewing in several towns, then you will need to do this for each one. Feel free to show your ID card, the "Why We Ask You" folder, and the respondent letter. It is often useful and reassuring to respondents to tell them that we are indeed registered with local authorities and they can feel free to call the Chamber of Commerce or local police station for confirmation. If the person wants a direct confirmation from Ann Arbor, suggest a collect call to the head of the Field Office at area code 313, 764-8356.

A standard form letter explaining the Center's work should already be on file with each of the local authorities mentioned above (Appendix C in this manual). However, it is a good idea to check back periodically to make sure they have ready access to the information. There may have been a turnover in staff or the information may have been misfiled; make sure the respondent will be given a favorable report by calling and checking up on us yourself.

Practice interviews. For most studies, every interviewer must take a practice interview *before* she begins to interview at the assigned addresses for the study. There are two reasons for requiring practice interviews: to familiarize the interviewer with the questionnaire in a working situation, and to help the supervisor, study directors, and the Field Office locate problems in the questionnaire in time to alert all interviewers about any trouble spots.

The best practice interviews are those taken with a "typical" respondent, i.e., one you do not know personally and whom you find by simply ringing a doorbell. Please do this whenever possible. Relatives and friends do not make good practice respondents.

After you have taken your practice interview and attended the prestudy conference, send the practice interview to your supervisor who will review it and return it to you with notes and comments.

Write "PRACTICE" on each practice interview so that it cannot be mistaken for a real interview. Be sure to attach your name label to the questionnaire or identify it positively in some other way.

Accounting for every sample address. The *green* Sample Address Summary Forms on which the assigned addresses from each sample segment have been listed are to be kept up-to-date by the FC as the primary area's master list (Illustration 11-11, page 85). Similarly, each interviewer who is not an FC should use the *white* summary sheets to record her own assigned addresses and to keep track of progress at each address. Unlisted HU's discovered during the course of interviewing should be added to these sheets if they fall on lines designated for sampling. Notify the Field Office of such HU's and report them to the FC so that they can be added to the primary area's master list. Each sample address should be visited early in the study period so that the interviewer will know what to expect at each address, and so that the FC's master list of sample addresses is complete at the earliest possible date.

You must keep your Sample Address Summary Form up-to-date for two reasons: to report your weekly progress to the FC, and to provide yourself with complete information as to when an interview was taken and mailed or what happened at an address classified as a nonresponse. Interviewers and FC's are expected to be able to report these items of information with ease for any address.

Numbering interviews. The Center guarantees the confidentiality of all information to respondents, and every effort is made to observe this pledge. Therefore, all direct identification, such as the address, is recorded on a cover sheet, which is detached from the interview after the sample listing has been accounted for in the Field Office. The interviewer's name and the interview number are used in the office to link the cover sheet, the interview, and associated forms.

Numbering your interviews is simple. The first completed interview you take on each study (after the practice interview) is interview number "1," the second one is number "2," the third is number "3," and so on. Enter this interview number on each interview questionnaire *and* on the cover sheet in the space provided. Keep a record of each interview number (and the address at which it was taken) on your copy of the Sample Address Summary Form.

Nonresponse cover sheets are not numbered. Each assigned line on a study must be accounted for with a cover sheet. If you were unable to take an interview, leave the space for "Your Interview Number" on the cover sheet blank. *Number only completed interviews.*

Mailing completed work to the Field Office. Each interviewer is responsible for mailing her own completed interviews and cover sheets to the Field Office; *never* give completed work to another person to mail for you. Interviews and cover sheets should be sent in from a post office or a box which you are certain has a regular pick up. NEVER HOLD COMPLETED INTERVIEWS LONGER THAN ONE WEEK. The Coding Section in Ann Arbor is designed to accommodate a steady flow of interviews from the field. Unless this flow is maintained, 20 or 30 coders will have little or nothing to do. By the same token, the coders cannot possibly do all the work required if the interviews arrive all at once. Please maintain or keep ahead of the mailing schedule on the progress report forms for each study.

Before you send any work to Ann Arbor, double check to be sure it is completed properly. Check to see that all necessary blanks are filled out on the cover sheets and questionnaires, and that all essential pieces of paper associated with an interview are enclosed, such as the cover sheet, recontact sheet, etc.

Do not staple anything; questionnaires must be separated from cover sheets and paper clips make this easier.

Use the large manila postpaid envelopes, preaddressed to the Field Office, to mail your interviews and cover sheets. Do not force too many completed interviews into one envelope, since heavier envelopes tend to become torn or damaged in the mails. Use one of your name labels on the envelope for your return address.

Mail all interviews and cover sheets First Class rather than Airmail unless otherwise instructed.

Since we pick up mail before the post office opens, Special Delivery does not speed arrival and may even cause delay.

Some interviewers like to insert a post card, self-addressed, in each envelope sent to the Field Office which contains interviews, listing the interviews enclosed. We date the cards on the day we receive them, and return them to the interviewers, so that they will not worry about whether or not the interviews reached the office. This procedure is not required; it is simply something the Field Office will do for the interviewer if she desires verification that her mail was received.

Study deadlines. Each study instruction book gives the starting and completion dates for interviewing. These dates are established by the Center, and are clearly specified both in the instruction book and on the availability memo sent to each interviewer before a study.

Deadlines allow about four days for the last interviews to arrive in the office. After that, the Coding Section closes down its operation, so it is most important that all interviews be in the mail by the deadline.

We all recognize that special circumstances — floods, snows, personal problems, etc. — may upset your best-laid plans. We only ask that you make allowances in your planning and not let things pile up toward the end of a study, and that when problems do arise, you let your supervisor and/or the Field Office know *immediately* so that provisions may be made or help provided. Occasionally an extension will be given by the Field Office if unusual situations arise.

Response rates. Interviewers can keep track of the response rate for their own portion of a study assignment. However, do not let your individual response rate interfere with your readiness to help other primary area staff members. The primary area is a unit, and the important response rate is the one that the whole primary area achieves, not one reached by any individual member of the primary area staff.

When we review response rates in the office, we realize that there are a number of circumstances which produce nonresponses through no fault of the interviewer. For example, there are respondents who move out of the country or die between waves of a panel study, respondents who are traveling or hospitalized for the entire study period, and people who are incapable of responding because of physical, mental, or language difficulties. We consider such cases "circumstantial" nonresponses.

Since these individuals are members of the sample population, for research purposes we must report them as nonresponses. Since they are unusual cases, they should not cause an interviewer to have a consistently low response rate from study to study, or even an unusually low response rate on a single study. We do not routinely distinguish between circumstantial nonresponses and other types, but, if there is ever a question as to the adequacy of an individual's or a primary area's response rate, we always go beyond the figures and examine the circumstances.

Tables for computing response rates and instructions for their use are provided at the end of this chapter (Appendix A).

STUDY MATERIALS

Questionnaires, instruction books, show cards, cover sheets, and other study materials are sent to the FC at the beginning of the study. We also send "Why We Ask You" folders, interviewer's cards, and postpaid envelopes if respondent letters are to be used.

If you are an FC, you should go over the study materials *as soon as they arrive* to see if all the necessary supplies have been included. This can be done quickly by checking actual quantities of materials against the checklist enclosed with each shipment.

Do not bother to return extra materials at the end of a study unless the Field Office requests that you do so. You should keep one or two copies of each item for your files and destroy the remainder.

Respondent letters. The following instructions apply if form letters are to be sent to respondents before interviewing.

- Put *your* initials or name over the return address in the upper left-hand corner of the envelope so that we will be able to return undeliverable letters directly to the interviewer who sent them.

- Address envelopes to "Residents of Household," *never* to "Occupant," and *never* to the respondent by name unless specifically instructed to do so.

- Type or print the address *neatly,* being sure to use the correct ZIP code.

We include enough letters and franked envelopes for you to send a letter to every assigned sample address and still have extra copies to show at the door or leave with a respondent who may not remember having received one.

"Why We Ask You" folders. This folder can be used at the door when you are explaining the purpose of the Center and the study, it can be left with the respondent when the interview has been completed, or it can be sent with respondent letters.

Interviewer's card. The interviewer's card was designed for multiple uses. There is enough room to write your name and a message on it if you find no one at home; it can serve as a calling card if you enclose it with the respondent letter, or you can leave it as a "thank you" card after an interview. Some respondents, particularly elderly ones, feel reassured if they know the name of the interviewer who has called on them.

Press release. If a press release is to be used, it will be collated in the back of the study instruction book. We have found that newspapers are likely to print these announcements only when they are personally delivered to an editor (the Business Editor is most likely to be interested in the quarterly economic studies). The FC should retype the release, including the names of the local interviewers working on the study and the approximate areas involved in the study. Some interviewers feel it is helpful to carry a clipping of this release as well as other news stories about surveys done by the Center when making household calls. We also like to receive these clippings in Ann Arbor — be sure to include the name of the paper and the date.

Interviewer's evaluation of the questionnaire. Please evaluate the questionnaire and procedures for each study on which you work; there will be a tear-out form for this purpose in the back of the study instruction book. Although new questions and new procedures are pretested before any national survey goes into the field, there are often difficult or awkward places of which only interviewers can be aware. Your comments will be tabulated along with those of other interviewers. In the past, these comments have been most helpful to us in improving the questions and questionnaire format.

Progress reports. Progress report forms for each study are sent with the study materials (Illustration 14-1). The FC should send these reports to her supervisor at the times printed on the report form — usually the same day every week. In accordance with this schedule, we suggest that interviewers and FC's establish a regular time for the interviewers to "report in" each week. For example, if the progress report must be mailed every Tuesday, the FC and interviewers might decide that 4:00-6:00 p.m. on Monday is a good

Illustration 14-1
PROGRESS REPORT

The University of Michigan
Survey Research Center   PROGRESS REPORT   MAIL TO YOUR SUPERVISOR ON
(Form revised 3/75)   (Second copy is for your files)

PRIMARY AREA _____   PROJECT NUMBER _____

Field Coordinator
for this study _____

	F.C.:	I'ER:	I'ER:	I'ER:	I'ER:	TOTAL
1. Total Number of Cover Sheets	____	+ ____	+ ____	+ ____	+ ____	= ____
2. Number of coversheets in nonresponse categories SLIP, HV, SV, VTS, or NER by study definition	____	+ ____	+ ____	+ ____	+ ____	= ____
3. SUBTRACT line 2 from line 1 and enter number of possible interviews	____	+ ____	+ ____	+ ____	+ ____	= ____
4. Number of interviews completed to date . .	____	+ ____	+ ____	+ ____	+ ____	= ____
5. Number of coversheets in nonresponse categories Ref, NOC(AT), RU, NI-Other which will remain so for the entire study .	____	+ ____	+ ____	+ ____	+ ____	= ____
6. ADD line 4 and line 5	____	+ ____	+ ____	+ ____	+ ____	= ____
7. SUBTRACT line 6 from line 3 to obtain the number of coversheets on which you are still working CHECK AGAINST COUNT OF REMAINING COVERSHEETS	____	+ ____	+ ____	+ ____	+ ____	= ____
8. Total cover sheets in lines 2 and 6 which have been MAILED to the Field Office . .	____	+ ____	+ ____	+ ____	+ ____	= ____
9. Percentage of coversheets MAILED to the Field Office (line 8 DIVIDED by line 1) If you are on schedule this will be the same or higher than _____ %						
10. Enter here the segment numbers assigned to each interviewer.		____	____	____	____	

119

time for the interviewers to call in. Once the schedule has been agreed upon, it is the responsibility of each interviewer to report her own progress to the FC, completely and promptly. Two copies of the progress report form are included in the back of the study instruction book for your use. Use one column for each week of the study rather than one for each interviewer.

Project completion form. Three copies of the project completion form are sent to each primary area at the beginning of each study (Illustration 14-2). As soon as all work on a study has been completed, the FC should fill out the form and send one copy to the Field Office, one copy to the supervisor, and keep one copy for the files. This will indicate that the primary area has completed the assignment, and that the last of the completed interviews and remaining cover sheets are in the mail. It is especially important for the Field Office to know that the FC considers all work completed in case there are discrepancies between the FC's records and the office records.

EVALUATION OF INTERVIEWERS

The objectives of the evaluation procedure are threefold:

• To monitor and control the quality of interviewing.

• To help interviewers develop their skills by providing feedback on their performance.

• To reward satisfactory performance by promotion (pay increase).

In line with the first two objectives, certain evaluation procedures are undertaken for each study, while the latter objective calls for a periodic review of the interviewer's progress in all phases of her work. The following is a summary of the procedures and forms used in evaluation.

Evaluation procedures for each study

• *Sample check.* When the Blue Folders and Sample Address Summary Sheets are returned to the office, the listings are reviewed by the Sampling Section to ensure their accuracy. The household listings and respondent selection procedures are checked by the Field Office when cover sheets are received. If there is information missing or if there are errors, the interviewer is contacted so that she can supply the information or correct the error. A copy of the office memo or telephone message is sent to the supervisor so that she will also be aware of the problem.

• *Response rates.* The response rate obtained on each study also plays a part in the evaluation procedure and becomes part of an interviewer's record. While it is important to obtain interviews from as many potential respondents as possible, quantity is only one indicator of performance. It should not overshadow the basic objective of getting the best possible data from the sample population. Interviewers may sometimes feel that they can improve their response rate by telling respondents that it will only take a few minutes and then rushing through the interview. This not only affects the quality of the information we receive, but antagonizes the respondent as well.

• *Coder's reports.* During the coding process, each interview is closely analyzed. Deficiencies noted by the coder are entered on an Interviewer Evaluation Card (Illustration 14-3), and given to the administrative assistant responsible for that study. The interviewer is informed of serious problems immediately so that corrective action can be taken, and less pressing problems, such as poor legibility, are noted if they seem to be a continuing problem.

If we receive a number of complaints from the Coding Section about a particular interviewer, the Field Office conducts a complete review of that interviewer's work.

• *Respondent evaluation letter.* Shortly after we begin receiving interviews on a study, we start sending evaluation letters to respondents (Illustration 14-4). The purpose of these letters is to find out from respondents how they felt about the interviews. Two of the questions in the letter are directly related to the interviewer's performance. About 20 percent of each interviewer's respondents will receive the letter. The response rate (the number of respondents filling out the form and returning it to us) is normally better than 50 percent. If we do not receive any replies from the set of one interviewer's respondents, we telephone those who did not respond and use the short evaluation questionnaire.

• *Nonresponse check by supervisors.* During periodic visits to their primary areas, supervisors either telephone or call in person at randomly selected noninterview addresses. This procedure is part of the continuing effort to study the differences between those who respond to our questions and those who do not.

• *Progress reports.* The last item that is part of the monitoring process is the weekly progress report sent from the Field Office to the supervisor. This report covers work *received* in the office, and is a companion to the report sent by the FC to the supervisor. We have found that

Illustration 14-2
PROJECT COMPLETION FORM

The University of Michigan
Survey Research Center

PROJECT COMPLETION FORM

Field Office
(Rev. 3/75)

Field Coordinator
for this study: _____

PSU: _____   PROJECT NO.: _____

	F.C.	I'ER:	I'ER:	I'ER:	Total:
1. Total number of cover sheets	___	+ ___	+ ___	+ ___	= ___
2. Number of cover sheets in nonresponse categories SLIP, HV, SV, VTS, or NER by study definition .	___	+ ___	+ ___	+ ___	= ___
3. Subtract "2" from "1" to obtain total number of possible interviews	___	+ ___	+ ___	+ ___	= ___
4. Enter here the number of interviews completed .	___	+ ___	+ ___	+ ___	= ___
5. Number of cover sheets in (NAH, RA, REF, NI-Other) nonresponse categories Ref, NOC(AT), RU and NI-Other	___	+ ___	+ ___	+ ___	= ___

6. As a check to make sure your entries are accurate, the figures entered in Items 4 and 5 should add up to the sa figure you have entered for Item 3. Then to obtain your final response rate, divide the figure in #4 by the fi entered in #3. $\dfrac{\text{"3"}}{\text{"4"}}$ *

*See Appendix A in the Interviewer's Manual for help in computing response rate.

MAIL ONE COPY TO YOUR SUPERVISOR AND ONE COPY TO FIELD OFFICE WITH FINAL COVER SHEETS ON OR BEFORE CLOSING DATE OF STUDY.

Illustration 14-3
CODER'S REPORT

INTERVIEWER EVALUATION

PROJECT # _____ LOG # _____ INTERVIEWER'S # _____ INTERVIEWER'S NAME _____

INTERVIEWER HAS PROBLEMS WITH:

☐ 1. Legibility

☐ 2. Skipped Q's. Q.# _____, _____, _____.

☐ 3. Insufficient or inappropriate answers Q.# _____, _____, _____.

☐ 4. Insufficient occupation data (describe) _____

☐ 5. Other "NO-NO's" _____

6. Overall rating: ☐ VERY GOOD   ☐ VERY BAD

COMMENTS:

Illustration 14-4
RESPONDENT EVALUATION LETTER

SURVEY RESEARCH CENTER

Dear Respondent:

A short time ago you were kind enough to give us an interview in connection with our recent study.

The success of these surveys depends largely upon how people feel about the interview and how well it is conducted. Therefore, we would like to have your comments in order to make interviews as interesting and pleasant as possible.

In order to help us, would you please answer the few questions on the back of this letter and use the self-addressed envelope to return the form.

We want to thank you again for participating in our study.

Sincerely,

Robert L. Kahn
Director

RLK:pv

INSTITUTE FOR SOCIAL RESEARCH
THE UNIVERSITY OF MICHIGAN
ANN ARBOR, MICHIGAN 48106

Illustration 14-4 (continued)

PROJECT NUMBER _____

PSU _____

SEG. & LINE # _____

PLEASE CHECK THE ANSWER TO EACH QUESTION WHICH COMES CLOSEST TO YOUR OWN OPINION.

1. How interesting was the interview?
   - ☐ Very interesting
   - ☐ Fairly Interesting
   - ☐ Not very interesting
   - ☐ Not at all interesting

   COMMENTS: _____
   _____

2. About how long was your interview?

   _____ (MINUTES)

3. How did you feel about the length of your interview?
   - ☐ Much too short
   - ☐ Too short
   - ☐ About right
   - ☐ Too long
   - ☐ Much too long

4. Do you feel you were able to express your opinions fully on the topics covered?
   - ☐ Yes   ☐ No

   COMMENTS: _____
   _____

5. How well did the interviewer conduct the interview?
   - ☐ Very well
   - ☐ Fairly well
   - ☐ Not very well
   - ☐ Not at all well

   COMMENTS: _____
   _____

6. How well did the interviewer explain the purpose of the study?
   - ☐ Very well
   - ☐ Fairly well
   - ☐ Not very well
   - ☐ Not at all well

   COMMENTS: _____
   _____

7. What suggestions do you have that would make an interview like this more pleasant?

If you do not remember the interview, please check this box ☐ and return the form.

superior work cannot be done at the last minute, and therefore we attend closely to the progress of work during the study period.

Periodic evaluation procedures

• *Taped and observational interviews.* Accuracy in sampling, efficient work habits, the ability to establish good respondent and community relations and to apply interviewing techniques skillfully, are all essential qualities for a social research interviewer. None of the measures of interviewer performance mentioned in the study-by-study review is a direct indicator of how well the interviewer performs the central task of conducting the interview. Our evaluation system would be seriously incomplete if it were not for the tape recorded and observational interviews which allow the interviewer, supervisor, and office to obtain an objective evaluation of the skill with which interviewing techniques are applied in actual practice. In Chapter 5 we discussed ways in which the interviewer could use tape recording to improve her own skills. We have also developed an objective coding procedure which allows us to measure improvement in an interviewer's performance from one study to the next and to see how one interviewer compares with others working on the same study. One important feature of this coding system is the recognition it gives to correct procedures. Unfortunately, because of the time constraints while a study is in the field, interviewers are more likely to receive feedback about problems than about their strong points. But with coded evaluations of tape recorded interviews, good techniques are scored and identified along with problem areas.

Because we feel that these evaluations are helpful, we would like to do many more of them than time and money permit. You will probably be asked to tape a few interviews each year, and our policy is that no pay increase will be approved without an opportunity for us to review a recent taped or observed interview. Since we have only a limited number of recorders, we must send them from one area to another. When a recorder is available in your area, we urge you to make rapid and full use of it. A copy of the Tape Recorded Interview Evaluation Code is included in this manual (Appendix D) for your examination.

• *Primary area visits.* Supervisors are expected to visit each of their primary areas twice a year. For the primary area visit, the supervisor will set up a conference with the local interviewers. Often this conference coincides with the pre-study conference. One of the purposes of this visit and conference is to give interviewers a more detailed picture of their performance in terms of overall quality, average costs, and expected response rates.

The supervisor may use this visit to conduct observational interviews (observing an interviewer conduct a production interview) as well as to discuss with individual interviewers the tape recordings they have made. Often the supervisor will request that several interviews be recorded and sent to her for coding shortly before this visit so that she can discuss them with the interviewer at the time of the individual conference. The supervisor will also check the primary area files as well as the Field Maps and Yellow Folders which are kept by the FC. In addition, the supervisor will probably conduct an on-site verification of sample listings and call on a sample of nonresponse addresses from recent studies.

Survey Research Center supervisors are the most direct link between the interviewer in the field and the Ann Arbor office and study staff. Since supervisors are experienced interviewers who are familiar with the primary areas and their interviewers, our supervisors can help improve performance by identifying problems and suggesting ways of solving them. They can also convey information and suggestions from interviewers to the Field Office in order to help us improve our questionnaires, study designs, and interviewing methods. The supervisor will tell the interviewers what she would like to cover during her visit. Interviewers can make these visits most fruitful by being prepared for the prestudy conference, having their practice interviews ready, and arranging their schedules to make maximum use of the time the supervisor is visiting in the primary area. If there is a difficult field sampling problem which should be dealt with in person, the interviewers should alert the supervisor so that she can set aside the necessary time. The supervisor can be most supportive if interviewers let her know what their needs are before her visit.

• *Evaluation for pay increase.* The pay schedule lists pay grade levels and hourly pay rates. Promotion from level to level is *not* automatic. When the experience points credited to an interviewer approach the number required for promotion to the next level, the Field Office sends a copy of the Evaluation Sheet to Determine Eligibility for Pay Rate Change (Illustration 14-5) to the supervisor. All of the information which is gathered on a continuing basis is considered in this evaluation. The supervisor is given a summary of recent cost figures, response rates, coder's reports and respondent reactions. She bases her evaluation of "interviewer behavior" on analyses of recent tape recorded interviews and field observations (see Observation Interview Report Form, Illustration 14-6). The quality of communication between interviewer, supervisor, and Field Office is also reflected on the supervisor's Evaluation Sheet (Illustration 14-5).

INTERVIEWER'S MANUAL

At the same time the supervisor is evaluating the interviewer, the Field Office also makes an evaluation concerning pay rate change, based on similar information and the experience they have had with the interviewer. After both evaluations are complete, they are compared. Usually they are in agreement, but if there are differences, a consensus decision is made.

Illustration 14-5
EVALUATION SHEET TO DETERMINE ELIGIBILITY FOR PAY RATE CHANGE

Survey Research Center
The University of Michigan

Copy to be returned to Field Office

Field Office 8/75

Date sent _____

EVALUATION SHEET TO DETERMINE INTERVIEWER ELIGIBILITY FOR PAY RATE CHANGE

To:_____(Supervisor)

According to our records, _____Primary Area_____
will soon meet the experience requirement necessary for advancement to Level_____.
Before an increase is awarded, all aspects of an interviewer's work are to be evaluated by the Field Office and Supervisor independently and agreement reached that the overall performance merits an increase. We have established the following guidelines to facilitate your evaluation. You are encouraged to discuss this evaluation with the interviewer using this form. Please advise the interviewer that, upon approval by the Field Office, the actual pay rate increase will be awarded only when the necessary experience points are recorded at the Field Office. Points are recorded only <u>after</u> the study on which they were earned is completed.

PROCEDURES TO FOLLOW:

1. Arrange to have the interviewer tape an interview on a current study if possible, or a non-production one if there is no study in the field at the time you receive this notice. She may tape several interviews and send you one of her choice, being sure to charge the time spent to a current or upcoming study.

2. Fill out an Observational Interview Report and its attached Tape-Recorded Interview Evaluation and code sheet.

3. Fill out this Evaluation Sheet to Determine Interviewer Eligibility for Pay Rate Change.

4. Send the Observational Interview Report with attached Tape-Recorded Interview Evaluation, code sheets and this evaluation sheet to the Field Office.

5. You may keep a copy of the tape or ask that the original be returned to you by the Field Office so that you can go over it with the interviewer during your next Primary Area visit.

6. In addition to the taped interview, your evaluation should be based on personal observations made during Primary Area visits.

INTERVIEWING BEHAVIOR

Observational Interview: P. # _____ Int. # _____

(Check one box for each quality)

	EXCELLENT	GOOD	FAIR	POOR	VERY SUB-STANDARD
QUESTION ASKING: (reads questions as written, follows skips)	☐	☐	☐	☐	☐
SPEECH: (reads slowly, enunciates clearly and has proper inflection when speaking)	☐	☐	☐	☐	☐
PROBING: (ability to elicit accurate and complete information through non-directive probes)	☐	☐	☐	☐	☐
VERBATIM RECORDING: (ability to take down actual responses in respondent's own words)	☐	☐	☐	☐	☐

(over)

Illustration 14-5 (continued)

GENERAL INTERVIEWER QUALITIES (Check one box for each quality)

	EXCELLENT	GOOD	FAIR	POOR	VERY SUB-STANDARD
RELATIONSHIP WITH RESPONDENTS: Relates well with all types of respondents. Treats blacks and whites, rich and poor, those with high and low education with equal respect.	☐	☐	☐	☐	☐
COMMUNITY RELATIONS: Develops and maintains good relations with resources groups and individuals, e.g., groups furnishing interviewing sites, better business bureaus, newspapers, planning agencies, etc. Represents the University well.	☐	☐	☐	☐	☐
CONCERN WITH CONFIDENTIALITY: Understands importance of protecting the respondent and upholds the Center's ethical standards.	☐	☐	☐	☐	☐
PREPARATION: Studies instructions carefully, reviews materials, asks perceptive questions at prestudy conference, anticipates situations which may arise in interviewing and is ready to handle them.	☐	☐	☐	☐	☐
EFFECIENCY: Well organized, plans work well, concerned with ways of reducing costs or efforts without reducing quality.	☐	☐	☐	☐	☐
COMMITMENT TO STANDARDS OF QUALITY: Professional approach to interviewing and study objectives, seeks to improve skills, desire to do outstanding work.	☐	☐	☐	☐	☐
SAMPLING: Handles sampling problems well, thorough about filling out folders, listings, cover sheets, etc.	☐	☐	☐	☐	☐
COOPERATION: Willingness to carry load even when difficult, positive response to requests and guidance.	☐	☐	☐	☐	☐
COMMUNICATION WITH SUPERVISOR: Faithful reporting of vital information regarding ability to handle assignment, lets you know of problems and difficulties.	☐	☐	☐	☐	☐
PROMPTNESS: Practice interviews, early start on studies, meets study deadlines, does not hold completed work.	☐	☐	☐	☐	☐
ABSENCE OF RESTRICTIONS: Is ready, willing and able to handle all assignments in the Primary Area. Has transportation, can work whenever it is necessary to contact respondents within the Primary Area.	☐	☐	☐	☐	☐
ADMINISTRATIVE FORMS AND PROCEDURES: Keeps good records, reports, time cards and vouchers properly filled out.	☐	☐	☐	☐	☐
OVERALL RATING OF INTERVIEWER:	☐	☐	☐	☐	☐

```
RECOMMENDATION FOR      ☐ Approved
PAY INCREASE:           ☐ Hold until the conditions noted in attached memo are met.
```

Illustration 14-6
OBSERVATION INTERVIEW REPORT

The University of Michigan
Survey Research Center

Field Office
(Revised 3/75)

Interviewer's Name _____   Supervisor's Name _____

Primary Area _____   Date _____

MODE (CHECK AS MANY AS APPLY)
- [ ] Taped
- [ ] Personal Observation

SITUATION
- [ ] Production ————————➤
- [ ] Practice or nonproduction field interview
- [ ] Role Playing (Use only for newly hired interviewers)

Project # _____
Int. # _____

Control # _____
(Entered by Office)

Describe the interview situation: _____

_____

_____

In addition to coding the taped interview, give a brief description of the interviewer's performance, including strengths and weaknesses, in each of the following areas:

1. (If observed by the supervisor) <u>Self identification</u> (professional manner, personal appearance, mention of name and <u>organization</u>; etc.)

_____

_____

2. (If observed by the supervisor) <u>Explaining the survey</u> (mention or omission of purpose, objectives, sampling procedures; adequacy of explanation; R's satisfaction with explanation; etc.)

_____

_____

3. <u>Question asking</u> (degree of accuracy in reading the questions; following proper skip sequence; instances of rephrasing. misreading; etc.)

_____

_____

_____

Illustration 14-6 (continued)

4. Speech (pace of delivery; manner and inflection in reading the questions; clarity of speech; etc.)

   _____

   _____

   _____

5. Use of nondirective probes (acceptability of probes used; instances of directive probes; etc.)

   _____

   _____

   _____

6. Coverage of question objectives (adequacy of coverage; instances of missed objectives; instances of over-probing; etc.)

   _____

   _____

   _____

7. Professional handling of the interview situation (degree of control; use of positive reinforcement; etc.)

   _____

   _____

   _____

8. Interviewer's attitude toward respondent's answers (professional attitude of neutrality and acceptance)

   _____

   _____

   _____

9. Written recording of interview (accuracy of verbatim recording; legibility; cross-references; thumbnail sketch; etc.)

   _____

   _____

   _____

APPENDIX A

TABLE FOR COMPUTING PERCENTAGES
(BASES 5 through 22)

BASE

5	6	7	8	9	10	11	12	13	14	15	16	17	18	19	20	21	22	RATE
20%	17%	14%	13%	11%	10%	9%	8%	8%	7%	7%	6%	6%	6%	5%	5%	5%	5%	1
40	33	29	25	22	20	18	17	15	14	13	13	12	11	11	10	10	9	2
60	50	43	38	33	30	27	25	23	21	20	19	18	17	16	15	14	14	3
80	67	57	50	44	40	36	33	31	29	27	25	24	22	21	20	19	18	4
100	83	71	63	56	50	45	42	38	36	33	31	29	28	26	25	24	23	5
	100	86	75	67	60	55	50	46	43	40	38	35	33	32	30	29	27	6
		100	88	78	70	64	58	54	50	47	44	41	39	37	35	33	32	7
			100	89	80	73	67	62	57	53	50	47	44	42	40	38	36	8
				100	90	82	75	69	64	60	56	53	50	47	45	43	41	9
					100	91	83	77	71	67	63	59	56	53	50	48	45	10
						100	92	85	79	73	69	65	61	58	55	52	50	11
							100	92	86	80	75	71	67	63	60	57	55	12
								100	93	87	81	76	72	68	65	62	59	13
									100	93	88	82	78	74	70	67	64	14
										100	94	88	83	79	75	71	68	15
											100	94	89	84	80	76	73	16
												100	94	89	85	81	77	17
													100	95	90	86	82	18
														100	95	90	86	19
															100	95	91	20
																100	95	21
																	100	22

HOW TO USE THESE TABLES TO COMPUTE PERCENTAGES

Response Rate:

1) Subtract the number of cover sheets in nonresponse categories SLIP, HV, SV, VTS, or NER from the total number of cover sheets. The remainder is the *"base."*

2) Look across the top of these pages to find the "base."

3) The number of interviews you have completed is the "rate." Look down the side of the page until you find the *rate*.

4) Follow the "base" column down the page and the "rate" row across the page and the figure you find where they intersect is your response rate.

5) For example, if you have a total of 16 cover sheets, one of which is a SLIP, your "base" is 15. Assume you have obtained 13 interviews. This is your "rate." The point at which these intersect shows you have obtained an 87 percent response.

6) Response rates for samples larger than 40 can be computed by dividing *both* the base and the rate by a constant (usually 2, 3, or 4) and using the quotients to enter in these tables.

Completion rates:

The procedure is the same except the total number of cover sheets is the "base" and the number you have completed action on and returned to Ann Arbor is the "rate."

INTERVIEWER'S MANUAL

TABLE FOR COMPUTING PERCENTAGES
(BASES 23 through 40)

BASE

23	24	25	26	27	28	29	30	31	32	33	34	35	36	37	38	39	40	RATE
4%	4%	4%	4%	4%	4%	3%	3%	3%	3%	3%	3%	3%	3%	3%	3%	3%	3%	1
9	8	8	8	7	7	7	7	6	6	6	6	6	6	5	5	5	5	2
13	12	12	12	11	11	10	10	10	9	9	9	9	8	8	8	8	8	3
17	17	16	15	15	14	14	13	13	13	12	12	11	11	11	11	10	10	4
22	21	20	19	19	18	17	17	16	16	15	15	14	14	14	13	13	13	5
26	25	24	23	22	21	21	20	19	19	18	18	17	17	16	16	15	15	6
30	29	28	27	26	25	24	23	23	22	21	21	20	19	19	18	18	18	7
35	33	32	31	30	29	28	27	26	25	24	24	23	22	22	21	20	20	8
39	37	36	35	33	32	31	30	29	28	27	26	26	25	24	24	23	23	9
43	42	40	38	37	36	34	33	32	31	30	29	29	28	27	26	26	25	10
48	46	44	42	41	39	38	37	35	34	33	32	31	31	30	29	28	28	11
52	50	48	46	44	43	41	40	39	37	36	35	34	33	32	32	31	30	12
57	54	52	50	48	46	45	43	42	41	39	38	37	36	35	34	33	33	13
61	58	56	54	52	50	48	47	45	44	42	41	40	39	38	37	36	35	14
65	63	60	58	56	54	52	50	48	47	45	44	43	42	41	39	38	38	15
70	67	64	62	59	57	55	53	52	50	48	47	46	44	43	42	41	40	16
74	71	68	65	63	61	59	57	55	53	52	50	49	47	46	45	44	43	17
78	75	72	69	67	64	62	60	58	56	55	53	51	50	49	47	46	45	18
83	79	76	73	70	68	66	63	61	59	58	56	54	53	51	50	49	48	19
87	83	80	77	74	71	69	67	65	63	61	59	57	55	54	53	51	50	20
91	87	84	81	78	75	72	70	68	66	64	62	60	58	57	55	54	53	21
96	92	88	85	81	79	76	73	71	69	67	65	63	61	59	58	56	55	22
100	96	92	88	85	82	79	77	74	72	70	68	66	64	62	61	59	58	23
	100	96	92	89	86	83	80	77	75	73	71	69	67	65	63	62	60	24
		100	96	93	89	86	83	81	78	76	74	71	69	68	66	64	63	25
			100	96	93	90	87	84	81	79	76	74	72	70	68	67	65	26
				100	96	93	90	87	84	82	79	77	75	73	71	69	68	27
					100	97	93	90	88	85	82	80	78	76	74	72	70	28
						100	97	94	91	88	85	83	81	78	76	74	73	29
							100	97	94	91	88	86	83	81	79	77	75	30
								100	97	94	91	89	86	84	82	79	78	31
									100	97	94	91	89	86	84	82	80	32
										100	97	94	92	89	87	85	83	33
											100	97	94	92	89	87	85	34
												100	97	95	92	90	88	35
													100	97	95	92	90	36
														100	97	95	93	37
															100	97	95	38
																100	98	39
																	100	40

APPENDIX B
PRETESTING

For most studies conducted by the Survey Research Center, there are a number of basic steps (Interviewer's Manual, Chapter 1): defining the study objectives; choosing the study design; selecting a sample; and constructing a questionnaire. At this point, interviewers become a part of the process and are asked to "pretest" or use the questionnaire, then give "feedback" to the study staff on how it works in the field. National studies usually involve at least two pretests. Often, the first one will be done locally (Detroit, Flint, Toledo) and the second one will test for possible regional differences by sampling other sections of the country, i.e. Northwest, South, Northeast, etc.

As a pretester, the interviewer has a special responsibility: thoughtful and considered reactions to each question, to the interview as a whole, and to the overall procedures are most important. Based on the results of and comments on the pretest interviews taken by interviewers, study staff, and Field Office personnel, the final instrument will be designed for production interviewing.

The pretesting process can be divided into two parts for the purpose of this discussion: pretesting in the field and the debriefing meeting.

PRETESTING IN THE FIELD

After you have been contacted by your supervisor or the Field Office to work on the pretest, you will receive a packet of materials containing the number of questionnaires you have been asked to pretest, plus an additional copy for your comments and a Pretest Length Report Form.

The time allowed for pretesting is usually very limited, so that you *must* read through the materials and get started immediately.

The respondents you interview for a pretest will vary, depending upon the population to be sampled for the national study. If the survey were a study of working women, for instance, you would be asked to pretest the questionnaire by interviewing only working women. However, since most of the studies done by the Survey Research Center use a national cross-section sample, you are usually asked to pretest the questionnaire on a "range" of respondents; that is, to try to talk to a variety of people from different age, education, income level, race, and sex groups. You can accomplish this by going into parts of your primary area where you are likely to find different kinds of respondents. DO NOT interview people you know. Respondents are much more likely to give unbiased opinions to a stranger, and friends tend to chat or argue with you about the wording of the questions, making it difficult to tell how long each section really takes.

No letters will have been sent, so that you will be making your calls "cold." Do keep your SRC Identification Card readily available to show to potential respondents; you will also find the "Why We Ask You" folders quite persuasive. *Do not* tell your respondent that this is a pretest. He needs to feel that the research is important if it is to be a reliable pretest. You might say something like: "We are doing a study of wide public interest, and we need your opinion on subjects that are important to all of us." At the end of the interview, you may leave your Interviewer's Card and a Report Request Card, just as you do in production interviewing.

If you are pretesting in what is normally considered a primary area, be sure that your respondents are selected from areas which do not fall into the Center's actual sample chunks. We do not want to pretest any household which has a chance of falling into our national cross-section on any given study.

Plan to do some of your pretesting in the early evening and on weekends, if necessary, to obtain interviews with the kind of people who may not be available at other times.

You will need a note pad to record lengthy comments during the interview, as well as to record summary notes afterwards while it is fresh in your mind. The study director may wish to hear which questions are causing problems and may ask you to tape record some or all of your pretests. You should, of course, write down the respondent's replies in the questionnaire and edit carefully.

Follow the questionnaire as it is written as closely as possible for the first couple of interviews. If a question does not work, we want to be sure that it is not because you are unfamiliar with the material. As soon as you feel comfortable with the questionnaire, feel free to be more flexible. And keep an open mind! Very often, a question we think cannot possibly work, works beautifully with respondents, and vice-versa. You should be a neutral observer; make every attempt not to let your own bias become apparent to the respondent. By the same token, try to give an unbiased report of your experience to the study director.

To pretest as thoroughly as possible, here are some points to keep in mind:

• Record the exact time for each interview and for each section of the interview. Study directors are working within tight budgets and every minute of interviewing time must be used to its best advantage. If you time each section, the study directors will have a clear picture of all the pieces and will be able to decide where cuts might be made.

- It is important to record the overall reaction of the respondent to the interview. Did he enjoy it? Did he find it interesting, or boring and repetitious? Were there specific areas of the topic under study that he wanted to talk about that we never asked about? Were there questions or sections which seemed threatening? (Which ones, and, is there a way we could have asked the same thing without upsetting him?)

- Each question should read smoothly and flow smoothly; there should be no breaks in continuity. Sometimes just rearranging phrases within a question or questions within a section or even changing the order of the sections will contribute to a smoother flow. Work cautiously with any question that seems to be asking about two things at once, those in which it is not clear to whom the "you" refers, and those which seem to cut across two dimensions, e.g., frequency ("how often") and amount ("how much").

- Skip instructions and arrows leading to contingency questions may be incorrect or missing in the pretest draft of the questionnaire. Be alert for confusing patterns and instructions. If you feel you are being skipped around a question or section and missing relevant information as a result, go ahead and ask the question(s); in severe cases call the Field Office for guidance. In all cases, record all of your changes in the questionnaires.

- While you are pretesting, give some thought to areas which will need to be covered in the question-by-question section of the instruction book. Interviewers talking to respondents need to know what the objective of the question is and how far to probe, but the members of the study staff have worked with these questions for so long that they may find it difficult to know what is needed in this respect.

- Be alert for the questions and particular words that cause the respondent to say, "What do you mean?" Unlike regular production interviewing, in which you are usually obliged to say, "Whatever it means to you," we would like to have you give an explanation or to try a different word. We would also like to find out, if possible, what the respondent thought we meant in the first place. If you do explain or reword a question or give a definition, write down exactly what you have said and put it into parentheses.

- As usual, any probes you use should be recorded in parentheses at exactly the point at which they occurred in the interview. Remember, once the study is in the field, you will only be allowed to use standard, nondirective probes. If you feel that you cannot meet a question objective without a directive probe, be sure to comment on this at the debriefing.

- On closed questions, are the appropriate alternatives provided, both in the check boxes *and* as part of the question? Watch for alternatives that sound similar and may be difficult to distinguish (e.g., B, C, D, and E). Watch for ambiguity in the alternatives, such as "fair" which respondents can interpret as either "so-so" or "just." Do the alternatives on the show cards match those in the questionnaire? Do you need or would you like a show card where none has been provided? If you feel that a closed question is not working, see what happens when you leave it open.

- When you have finished pretesting, analyze your interviews in terms of your experience. Did certain questions always seem to get a "don't know" answer? Was it necessary to repeat certain questions because the respondent did not understand the words you used, or because the question was too long, or because the directions were unclear? Was the respondent frustrated because he did not get to say how he really felt about the topic? Sometimes the respondent will give you a good clue as to his feelings at the end of the interview; when you have closed your questionnaire and are collecting your pencils, he may make a comment such as, "That's all very well, but you didn't ask me about _____."

- Write a full thumbnail sketch on each interview, just as you do for a production interview, noting any unusual circumstances which might have affected the answer or which would explain why the respondent has answered the questions as he has. If you are not using a cover sheet, use the thumbnail to note the race, sex, age, education, and estimated income of the respondent.

- Do your editing as soon as possible after each interview. Make note of the problems and question numbers on a yellow pad. When you have completed the number of pretest interviews required, combine all of these comments in your comment copy of the questionnaire and be prepared to bring them up at the debriefing. Be sure to fill in the Pretest Length Report.

THE DEBRIEFING

The debriefing meeting is attended by a representative of the Field Office, the interviewers who have done the pretesting, members of the study staff, and often a representative from the Coding Section. Each has a responsibility:

- **The representative from the Field Office** usually chairs the meeting and is especially concerned with the mechanics of the questionnaire and its development into a format which the interviewers have been trained to use.

- **The interviewers** are responsible for pointing out problem areas and making suggestions for improvement.

- **The study staff** has overall responsibility for making sure the questionnaire meets the research objectives and for making final decisions about changes in the questionnaire.

- **The representative from the Coding Section** can help detect and alter any questions which may be interesting but which will be difficult to code and analyze systematically.

After introductions have been made, the study director may talk about the background of the study. Then each interviewer in turn will give a quick thumbnail of general impressions. While this is being done, the Pretest Length Reports will be collected and a tabulation made, which will be followed by a question-by-question discussion of the questionnaire. Your comment copy will be helpful in quickly spotting those areas which caused problems. You will also need to refer to your completed interviews, especially if the study staff is interested in the distribution of answers on particular questions.

Please speak out; the study staff will welcome your constructive suggestions, but do not be crushed if it does not accept all of your advice. Sometimes particular sets of questions or the wording of a question cannot be changed because of research objectives, methodology, or because they have been included for trend or replication purposes. For example, the first set of questions about business conditions and consumer intentions on the quarterly economic studies are questions which cannot be changed. Often these questions will have an asterisk in the pretest questionnaire to warn the interviewer not to waste time or energy trying to change them.

At the end of the debriefing session the questionnaires will be collected for further study and analysis by the study staff. Often, crucial questions or sets of questions will be coded and tabulated to see if interviewers obtained the range of response that was expected.

Note: For national pretests, the debriefing session is usually done by telephone, either with each interviewer separately or through a conference call with all the pretest interviewers and study staff participating. In some cases we may just ask the interviewers to mail their interviews along with their written comments.

PRETESTING ELITES

Occasionally the Survey Research Center undertakes a survey which is interested in a special sample of respondents, such as convention delegates, government officials, judges, doctors, etc. This kind of sample population is often referred to as an "elite" sample.

Pretesting an instrument to be used in interviewing an elite sample presents some different kinds of challenges to the pretest interviewer. First, you will not be able to go out and ring doorbells until you find a suitable subject; instead, either you or the study staff must set up interviews with respondents who meet the sample requirements but who cannot fall into the population to be sampled on the regular study. Second, there may be extensive use of technical language in the questionnaire which the study staff and the respondents understand, but with which you may be unfamiliar. This makes probing more difficult, since you may not be sure if the respondent has answered the question or just talked around it. For questionnaires of this kind, we need your help in compiling a glossary of terms for the interviewers' use and suggestions for the study instruction book.

You will find the tape recorder an important aid in this kind of pretesting, since knowledgeable respondents are apt to talk long and fast about their topic. Used in combination with the verbatim written record, a tape gives the study staff the flavor of the interviewing situation and is an invaluable help to the interviewer in editing.

APPENDIX C
LETTER TO AUTHORITIES

SURVEY RESEARCH CENTER

INSTITUTE FOR SOCIAL RESEARCH

THE UNIVERSITY OF MICHIGAN

ANN ARBOR, MICHIGAN 48106

TO WHOM IT MAY CONCERN:

From time to time representatives of The University of Michigan's Survey Research Center will be taking some interviews in your area. In answer to any inquiries you may receive about us from people in your community, regarding our interviewers and the authenticity of our surveys, below is a brief description of our work.

Each year since 1946 the Survey Research Center has carried out nationwide interview surveys designed to get an accurate picture of how American people are getting along these days, and how they feel about economic conditions, as well as other important matters. Our program of research is carried on under government, industrial, and foundation sponsorship - the requirements being that the projects be scientifically valuable, socially worthwhile, and that the results be available for public use.

This area is one of 74 sample points maintained throughout the country. Addresses at which interviews are to be taken within each area are randomly selected by scientific sampling procedures, to represent an accurate cross-section of the nation. Results of all the interviews are combined and published in reports which represent the country as a whole. These reports are statistial and no person is ever identified. Interviews are held in strict confidence here at The University.

Since our present schedule of work involves a new study every few months, we hope this letter may serve as a permanent notification of our ongoing activity in your area. A local representative will notify you periodically of new studies so that you may be alerted to current surveys. The accompanying letter lists the names of our local staff members, each of whom has been specially trained in interviewing and sampling procedures, and carries proper identification as an employee of The University of Michigan.

Should you wish additional information about our organization, the persons listed in the attached letter will answer any inquiries, or you may contact me directly.

Sincerely,

John C. Scott
Head, Field Section

JCS:mb
encl.

APPENDIX D
TAPE-RECORDED INTERVIEW EVALUATION CODE

CODE	BEHAVIOR — desirable	CODE	BEHAVIOR — undesirable
11	Reads question exactly as written.	21	Reads stem exactly, but not choices.
12	Makes slight change which does not alter frame of reference; choices read exactly; no key words added, omitted, or changed.	22	Reads question incorrectly; reads only part of question; any key word added, omitted, or changed.
		23	Assumes answer to question which may have been asked in the form of a statement. (And you rent this apartment.) *Some* verbal behavior occurs. (See code 93.)
14	Good, deliberate pace; R understands question first time it is read.	24	Pace too rapid; R does not understand; asks for repeat of Q.
31	Makes up nondirective probe. (Anything else? Could you repeat that? Could you tell me more about that?)	41	Makes up directive probe. (That's all? Nothing else?)
32	Repeats question or part of question and/or choices correctly.	42	Repeats question and/or choices incorrectly; reads only part of choices when should read all; incorrect summary of R's answer; interprets R's answer.
33	Phrases introduction to a section in a nondirective manner.	43	Phrases introduction to a section in a directive manner.
34	Repeats R's response or part of it correctly; correct summary of R's response.	45	Incorrect confirmation; interprets question; volunteers clarification.
35	Confirms frame of reference for R; gives clarification only in response to request for it. (Whatever "good" means to you. R: Does the attic bedroom count? I'er: Yes.)	46	Fails to probe after inadequate response.
36	Probes after inadequate response.	47	Fails to probe initial DK when appropriate.
37	Probes an initial DK when appropriate.		
51	Helps R to understand his role. (We are interested in your opinions.)	62	Interrupts R.
52	Slight paraphrasing of R's response but does not affect meaning.	63	Gives personal opinion; indicates agreement or disagreement with R; praises or criticizes R; gives unacceptable feedback; shows or expresses surprise or displeasure.
53	Reinforces R's desirable behavior with nod, smile, uh-huh, ignores undesirable behavior.	65	Illegible; not edited to readable standard.
55	Legible; easy to read.	66	Does not record R's relevant remarks on precoded questions.
57	Records response and/or own words correctly and completely.	67	Records response and/or own words incorrectly or incompletely.
58	Makes other acceptable remarks. (Would you like me to reread this? Do you want me to stop while you get the boys' lunch?) Instructions in use of show card.	68	Makes other unacceptable remarks. (Now I have to go to page 10.)
81	Skips question correctly.	92	Skips question incorrectly.
84	Marks INAPS so that I'w is easy to follow.	93	Records answer from previous answer or inference; no verbal behavior occurs.
85	Makes good marginal comments and cross references.	94	Does not mark INAPS.
		98	Missing data; unknown; no sound on tape.

INDEX

A

Abbreviations, 22-23
Apartment buildings: how to list, 45-46, 80; vs. institutions, 47
Apartment (residential) hotels defined, 46
Appointments, 29
Area listing procedure: described, 41; how to use, 47-59; when to use, 44-45
Area segments: checking, 86; defined, 77
Authorities, contacting local, 116
Availability forms, 115

B

Bias, 7
Blue Folder: back cover, 66; contents, 66; cover, 65-66; described, 65; inside spine, 66; use after listing, 83-84
Boundaries: checking, 42-43, 77-78; civil, 43; nonexistent, 44; selecting, 48-49; vs. number of HU's, 44
Building listing procedure: described, 41; how to use, 59-64; when to use, 45
Building Listing Sheet, 41, 59, 60-64
Building segments: checking, 86-87; defined, 77-78

C

Callback procedure, 29
Chunk: boundaries, 42-44; defined, 37; map vs. sketch, 42; scouting materials, 41; selection, 37
Clarification, as a probe, 16
Coder's report, 120
Conferences, prestudy, 115-116
Confidentiality, 4, 116-117
Correspondence with Field Office, 113
Cover Sheet: how to use, 77; information to list, 23; when to use, 29, 84
Cross references in write-up, 22

D

Deadlines, 117
Deductions. See Payroll Practices.
Descriptive statistical survey, 2

E

Editing interviews, 22, 25, 28
Escorts, 110
Evaluation: by interviewer, 28, 118; of interviewer, 120, 125-126
Evaluation Sheet to Determine Eligibility for Pay Rate Change, 125
Excluded living quarters: defined, 40; exceptions within, 40; institutional, 40; listing, 46, 83; transient or seasonal, 40
Expense report. See Travel Expense Report.
Expenses, 109-111

F

Family relationships, determining, 94-95
Family unit defined, 94
Feedback, 13-14
Field Coordinator's role, 114-115
Field Office: address and telephone, 113; when to contact, 114
Folders: Blue, 65-66; Yellow, 66, 77
Forms. See individual listings.

H

Hotels: apartment, 46; for transients, 47; listing, 82
Household: composition, 91, 94-95; head of, 95; members of, 93
Housing units: counting, 47; defined, 39-40; direct access to, 39; estimating, 49, 60; examples of, 40; identifying occupied, 91; identifying unique, 39; in multi-unit buildings, 79; in nonresidential buildings, 81; kitchen facilities in, 39; listing, 78-83, 87; number of families in, 39; selection of, 37; substitution, 37; temporarily in nonresidential use, 81; under construction, 81; vacant or dilapidated, 81; vs. boundaries, 44

I

Identification card, 7
Immediate Action Memos, 30, 113
Inappropriate questions, 22-23
Information Sheet: completing after scouting, 50, 64; illustration, 50, 53, 55-56
Institutional living quarters: listing, 82; to be excluded, 40; vs. apartments, 47
Insurance, 110-111
Interpreters, 110
Interview: coding, 4-5; editing, 22, 25, 28; identifying, 23, 116; overview, 4; practice, 116; securing, 7-9; tape recorded, 25, 28; transcribing, 19
Interviewer: card, 30, 118; comments in write-up, 22; evaluation by, 28, 118; evaluation of, 120, 125-126; initial contact by, 7; manner of, 11; time sheets, 101-102; work hours, 101-102

L

Letters: persuasion, 30-31, 99; respondent, 7, 116, 118; to authorities, 116

Listing: area procedure described, 41; building procedure described, 41; choosing a procedure, 44-45; families, 95; perfecting, 86-90; segments, 77-79; types of living quarters, 80-83; use of in interviewer evaluation, 120

Living quarters, 39-40, 80-82

M

Map: field, 41; for sample locations, 65; illustration, 50, 52; inaccurate, 44; scale, 42; symbols, 42; vs. sketch, 42

Market research survey, 2

Materials: listing, 65; received from Ann Arbor office, 41; returning to Ann Arbor office, 50, 64, 84, 117; scouting, 41; study, 115, 118. *See also* Supplies.

Meals, compensation for, 111

Mileage: reimbursement for, 102, 109-111; Statement, 102

Military reservations, 82

N

Noninterview, 97

Nonresponse: check by supervisors, 120; cover sheets, 117; status categories, 97-99; summary categories, 99

Note taking, 21-22

O

Observational interview, 125

Occupancy, determining, 91

Office forms and records: copies, 101; use of ink, 101; when to submit, 101

Oversized segments, 83

P

Parking, compensation for, 109

Payroll practices, 111

Pencil, use of number two, 22, 41, 59

Personal data, gathering, 13

Persuasion letter, 30-31, 99

Population. *See* Sample.

Postage, compensation for, 109-110

Press release, handling, 118

Prestudy conferences described, 115-116

Pretesting, 133-135

Primary area: defined, 35; files, 115; selection, 35; supervisor visits, 125

Probes: abbreviations for, 16; directive, 17; examples of, 17-18; functions of, 15; including in notes, 21; kinds of, 15-16; nondirective, 16-17; skillful use of, 16

Progress reports, 118-120, 125

Project Completion Form, 120

Public opinion poll, 2

Q

Questionnaire: constructing and pretesting, 4, 133-135; design of Survey Research Center, 11; format and conventions, 19; general use of, 11-14

Questions: asking, 11; changing wording of, 11, 13; check-off, 19; closed, 19-20; neutral, as probes, 16; often asked by respondents, 8-9; omitting, 12; open-ended, 19; order of presentation, 12; reading pace for, 12; repeating, 12-13, 15; restricted, 19; unrestricted, 19; write-in, 19

R

Racial composition of segments, 49

Raises. *See* Payroll Practices.

Receipts for expenses, 102, 109

Recording responses during interview, 20-23

Relisting while checking segments, 86

Report writing, 5

Respondent: letter, 7, 116, 118; questions, 8-9; reasons for refusal, 31; reluctant, 30-31; role in interviewer evaluation, 120; selecting, 92-97

Response: cross referencing, 22; editing, 22, 25; inadequate, 15; rates, 117-118, 120; recording, 20-22; repeating, 15-16

Results, tabulating and analyzing, 5

Rooming houses, 82

S

Sample, selection of, 3, 35-37

Sample Address Summary Form, 77, 84, 116

Sampling, 35, 37

Scouting, 41-64. *See also* Listing; Respondent, selecting

Seasonal living quarters: excluded, 40; listing, 46, 82; occupancy, 92

Segment: boundaries, 48-49; defined, 37, 77-78; identification, 41; listing procedures, 77-79; listing sheets, 77, 78, 86; racial composition of, 49; selection, 37

Selection Table, 95-97

Single-family houses, 80

Sketch: illustrations, 50, 54, 57, 58; internal features in, 44; scale, 42; symbols in, 42; updating, 43, 47, 49; vs. map, 42

Skipped questions, 23

Social research survey, 2

Stratification, 35
Study: deadlines, 117; design, 3; materials, 115, 118; objectives, 3; procedures, 115. *See also* Survey.
Supervisor, 114
Supplies, 109. *See also* Materials.

⋯gy, 3-5; origins, 2; ⋯ of, 1, 2. *See also* Study.

⋯ing, 28; for interviewer ⋯5, 28; telephone, 28, 34;

⋯ contact with Field ⋯nterviews, 33-34; tape ⋯ use for initial contact,

⋯ compensation for,

⋯h of, 46, 58, 59
⋯ded, 40; hotels, 47;

Transmittal Form, 41, 50, 51
Transportation, compensation for, 109, 111
Travel Expense Report, 102, 109-111

U

Unclassified living quarters, 40, 83

V

Vacancy: determining, 91; listing for housing units, 81, 83; listing for trailer parks, 81; seasonal, 92

W

"Why We Ask You" Folder, 116, 118

Y

Yellow Folder, 66, 77

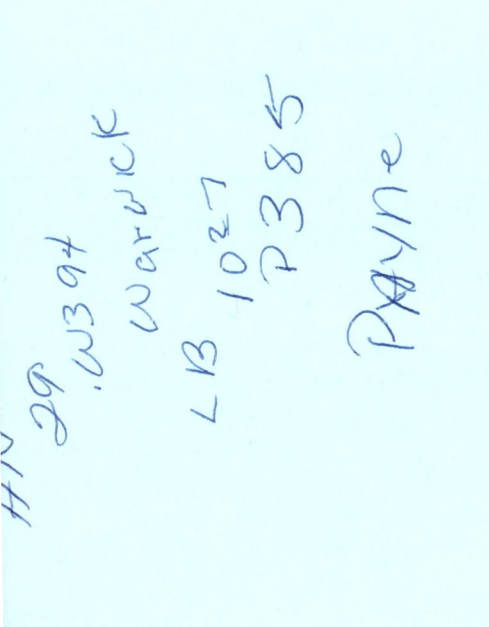

143

Volumes on Research Methodology from the Institute for Social Research

MEASURES FOR PSYCHOLOGICAL ASSESSMENT: A Guide to 3,000 Original Sources and Their Applications by Ki-Taek Chun, Sidney Cobb, and John R.P. French, Jr. 1975. 688 p.

A TECHNIQUE FOR EVALUATING INTERVIEWER PERFORMANCE: A Manual for Coding and Analyzing Interviewer Behavior from Tape Recordings of Household Interviews by Charles F. Cannell, Sally A. Lawson, and Doris L. Hausser. 1975. 138 p.

DATA PROCESSING IN THE SOCIAL SCIENCES WITH OSIRIS by Judith Rattenbury and Paula Pelletier. 1974. 245 p.

A GUIDE FOR SELECTING STATISTICAL TECHNIQUES FOR ANALYZING SOCIAL SCIENCE DATA by Frank M. Andrews, Laura Klem, Terrence N. Davidson, Patrick O'Malley, and Willard L. Rodgers. 1974, second printing 1975. 36 p.

SEARCHING FOR STRUCTURE by John A. Sonquist, Elizabeth Lauh Baker, and James N. Morgan. 1971. Revised edition 1974. 236 p.

INTRODUCTION TO THE IBM 360 COMPUTER AND OS/JCL (JOB CONTROL LANGUAGE) by Judith Rattenbury. 1971. Revised edition 1974. 103 p.

MULTIPLE CLASSIFICATION ANALYSIS: A Report on a Computer Program for Multiple Regression Using Categorical Predictors by Frank M. Andrews, James N. Morgan, John A. Sonquist, and Laura Klem. 1967. Revised edition 1973. 105 p.

MEASURES OF SOCIAL PSYCHOLOGICAL ATTITUDES by John P. Robinson and Phillip R. Shaver. 1969. Revised edition 1973. 750 p.

MEASURES OF OCCUPATIONAL ATTITUDES AND OCCUPATIONAL CHARACTERISTICS by John P. Robinson, Robert Athanasiou, and Kendra B. Head. 1969, sixth printing 1974. 480 p.

MULTIVARIATE NOMINAL SCALE ANALYSIS: A Report on a New Analysis Technique and a Computer Program by Frank M. Andrews and Robert C. Messenger. 1973, third printing 1975. 114 p.

THAID: A Sequential Analysis Program for the Analysis of Nominal Scale Dependent Variables by James N. Morgan and Robert C. Messenger. 1973, second printing 1974. 98 p.

OSIRIS: Architecture and Design by Judith Rattenbury and Neal Van Eck. 1973, second printing 1974. 315 p.

ECONOMIC SURVEY METHODS by John B. Lansing and James N. Morgan. 1971, fourth printing 1974. 448 p.

INFERENCE FROM SURVEY SAMPLES: An Empirical Investigation by Martin R. Frankel. 1971, fourth printing 1974. 173 p.

MULTIVARIATE MODEL BUILDING: The Validation of a Search Strategy by John A. Sonquist. 1970, third printing 1975. 264 p.

The above listed volumes are published by the Institute for Social Research. For information about prices and available editions write to: Sales Fulfillment Section, Institute for Social Research, The University of Michigan, Box 1248, Ann Arbor, Michigan 48106.